Speaking CAE

Ten practice tests for the **Cambridge C1 Advanced**

Luis Porras Wadley

PROSPERITY EDUCATION

PROSPERITY EDUCATION
www.prosperityeducation.net

Registered offices: Sherlock Close, Cambridge
CB3 0HP, United Kingdom

© Prosperity Education Ltd. 2021

First published 2021

ISBN: 978-1-91-382544-7

This publication is in copyright. Subject to statutory exception and to the provisions of relevant collective licensing agreements, no reproduction of any part may take place without the written permission of Prosperity Education.

'Cambridge C1 Advanced' and 'CAE' are brands belonging to The Chancellor, Masters and Scholars of the University of Cambridge and are not associated with Prosperity Education or its products.

The moral rights of the author have been asserted.

Cover design and typesetting by ORP Cambridge

For further information and resources, visit:
www.prosperityeducation.net

To infinity and beyond.

Contents

Introduction	4
Cambridge C1 Advanced: Speaking parts	5
Frequently asked questions	6
Test 1	9
Test 2	17
Test 3	25
Test 4	33
Test 5	41
Test 6	49
Test 7	57
Test 8	65
Test 9	73
Test 10	81
Model answers	89
Examiner's comments	95
Part 2 booklet (colour) download code	100

Introduction

The C1 Advanced examination, formerly known as the Advanced Certificate in English (CAE), is an examination developed by Cambridge Assessment English, which is part of the University of Cambridge.

The C1 Advanced is usually taken by candidates who want to obtain a C1-level certificate, which corresponds to an advanced level of English. As described by the Common European Framework of Reference for Languages (CEFRL), candidates with a C1 level are considered *proficient users* with *effective operational proficiency*, thus being able to:

- understand a wide range of demanding, longer texts, and recognise implicit meaning
- express themselves fluently and spontaneously without much obvious searching for expressions
- use language flexibly and effectively for social, academic and professional purposes
- produce clear, well-structured and detailed texts on complex subjects, showing controlled use of organisational patterns, connectors and cohesive devices.

The Speaking paper is one of the five papers that comprise the C1 Advanced examination. This section of the exam is taken in pairs, or trios, of candidates, who are assessed by two examiners: the interlocutor and the assessor. The interlocutor is responsible for delivering the instructions, handling the test booklet and interacting with the candidates, while the assessor simply listens and marks each candidate's performance.

The Speaking paper is divided into four parts, all of which comprise a different task. Different degrees of participation are expected from the candidates in each of these tasks.

This book aims to provide meaningful speaking practice while following the format of the C1 Advanced Speaking paper. Both teachers and candidates can benefit from this resource, in that they can familiarise themselves with the format and level of the exam, and the type of questions and topics covered. Furthermore, and most importantly, students can learn, through repetitive practice, what to expect on the day of their Speaking exam.

I hope that you will find this resource a useful study aid, and I wish you all the best in preparing for the C1 Advanced examination.

Luis Porras Wadley

Granada, 2021

Luis Porras Wadley is the owner and director of KSE Academy, an English academy and official Cambridge Exam Preparation Centre based in Granada. As an English teacher, Luis has been preparing Cambridge candidates successfully more than ten years.

C1 Advanced: Speaking parts

In **Part 1**, candidates are asked questions mainly about themselves, their background and their experiences. It starts with a set of brief introductory questions (e.g. *...and your names are? Where are you from?*) and continues with one or more topic-based questions. These topics may include things like holidays and travel, leisure-time activities, friends and family, television, etc. In responding to these questions, candidates are expected to provide brief but complete answers.

Timing	2 minutes (pair) / 3 minutes (trio)
Focus	Giving personal information, expressing opinions about various topics and talking about past experiences and plans for the future.
Interaction	Interlocutor – Candidate

In **Part 2**, each candidate is asked to talk about two out of three photographs and also to answer a question about their partner's photographs. Each candidate must compare a pair of pictures and answer two questions about those pictures in one minute. Following this, the other candidate is asked a different question related to the pictures themselves or the topic of the pictures (thirty seconds). The three photographs and the questions are different for each candidate.

Timing	4 minutes (pair) / 6 minutes (trio)
Focus	Describing, comparing, expressing opinions and speculating.
Interaction	Interlocutor – Candidate

Part 3 is the main collaborative task of the test. In this part, candidates are presented with a topic in the form of a question (e.g. *Why might these career paths be popular at present?*) and a few prompts linked to it (e.g. *healthcare, higher education, digital marketing,* etc.). The candidates are then expected to develop a two-minute discussion around the topic, making use of the prompts provided. When the two minutes are up, they are asked to make a decision with regard to the topic (e.g. *...decide which field will become most popular among young people in the near future.*). The candidates have one more minute to complete the task.

Timing	4 minutes (pair) / 6 minutes (trio)
Focus	Discussing, exchanging ideas, agreeing and disagreeing, asking for opinions, explaining views, justifying opinions, reaching agreements, making decisions, etc.
Interaction	Interlocutor – Candidate – Candidate

In **Part 4**, candidates are asked some questions that stem from the discussion topic in Part 3. These are questions that normally touch on complex issues such as education, learning, work, healthy habits, careers, new technologies, etc. The candidates are expected to develop extended answers, and may be prompted to exchange views rather than answer individually.

Timing	5 minutes (pair) / 8 minutes (trio)
Focus	Exchanging ideas, extending and explaining answers, agreeing/disagreeing and justifying opinions.
Interaction	Interlocutor – Candidate – Candidate

Cambridge C1 Advanced: Speaking

Is the Speaking test taken individually or in pairs? The Speaking test is taken in pairs or trios, unless a candidate has special needs that may affect their performance. This may lead to them taking the test individually. However, regular tests are normally taken in pairs, and if there is an uneven number of candidates, only the last three candidates will take the test as a trio.

How long is the Speaking test? Normally, the Speaking exam will last around 15 minutes. However, when taken as a trio, the test will last around 23 minutes, so that all candidates have the same chance to speak as if they were in a regular pair-format test.

Can candidates choose to do the test with a friend or classmate? This depends on the examination centre candidates register with. Each centre has its own policies and so this may or may not be allowed. In the end, it is up to the supervisor of the exam session to allow it or not, and the decision will be based on exam timing and logistics rather than candidates' preferences.

Do candidates have to speak with each other at some point? Yes, they do. Candidates must always speak to each other in Part 3 and will usually do so in Part 4. The rest of the test is carried out individually yet, in their answers, candidates can refer to what the other candidate has said earlier in the test.

How many people are there in the examination room? In the examination room there can be up to five people: two examiners and two or three candidates. Occasionally, there may be a third examiner, but their role will not be to assess the candidates.

What happens if the interlocutor interrupts a candidate when the time allocated to a task is up? This is completely normal, and candidates should expect to be interrupted when the time is up. The interlocutor's job involves ensuring that every candidate has the same opportunities to speak, which includes having the same time allocated to do so. If a candidate has developed their answer well and has responded fully, but with time to spare, they will not lose marks.

In Part 2, do candidates need to specify the pictures that they are going to compare? No, this is not necessary. It is common for candidates to begin their turn with something like *"I'm going to talk about the first and the third picture"*. However, this is not necessary and it takes time from the 60 seconds the candidate has in which to compare the pictures and answer the questions. Examiners will easily know which pictures the candidate is referring to from the content of their speech, and, also, candidates can point to the pictures while talking about them to clarify the ones to which they are referring.

What do candidates need to take with them to the Speaking test? Candidates need to take a valid form of photographic ID (Passport, National Identity Card, Driver's Licence, etc.) and their Confirmation of Entry, which is a document provided by the examination centre some time before the test.

In Part 3, must candidates reach an agreement by the end of the task? Not at all. The purpose of the test is to assess candidates' speaking skills, not the completion of the task or the conveyance of their opinions. Candidates are only expected to develop a discussion in which they work towards an agreement or decision by means of exchanging views and opinions, and agreeing and disagreeing. Whether or not they have reached an agreement by the end of the task is irrelevant to the awarding of their mark.

In Part 3, do candidates have to talk about all the different prompts? No, this is not necessary. The prompts in this part of the test are there to ensure that candidates have some ideas to talk about and that they engage in a discussion. However, they are not necessarily expected to use all of them, nor are they limited to those prompts; they can bring their own ideas into the discussion.

Frequently asked questions

What are the mark sheets mentioned at the beginning of the exams? The mark sheets contain each candidate's name, surname and their candidate number, and this is where the assessor writes their marks. These sheets are given to candidates before they enter the examination room, and they will have to give them to the interlocutor at the beginning of the test. The examiners will then keep the mark sheets to relay the candidates' marks to Cambridge Assessment English.

Where does the Speaking exam take place? The Speaking exam can take place in a range of venues, but it is most likely to take place in the examination centre itself (usually a language school) or one of its examination venues, which also tend to be language schools and, sometimes, hotels or conference rooms.

Is the Speaking exam done the same day as the other parts of the test? Not normally, but it can happen. Given the length of the whole exam, it is usually more practical and reasonable to do the Speaking test on a different day. This is decided by the examination centres and candidates are informed of this well in advance.

Will the examiners be looking at the candidates throughout the whole test? No, they will not. Examiners, especially the assessors, have to assign marks while the exam is taking place. For this reason, there will be times throughout the test when they might be looking at their examiner booklets or candidate mark sheets instead of the candidates. However, this does not mean that they are not paying attention to the candidates and their responses!

How is the Speaking exam marked? Each candidate's performance throughout the test is marked both by the interlocutor and the assessor, who give candidates a score for six different categories: grammatical resource, lexical resource, discourse management, pronunciation, interactive communication and global achievement. The assessor is responsible for assessing the first five categories, which account for two thirds of the score, and the interlocutor awards the global mark, which comprises one third of the final speaking score.

Can another candidate's performance affect a candidate's score? No, it cannot. Although the exam is taken in pairs or trios, candidates are assessed individually and examiners are duly trained to do so, ensuring that both candidates have the same opportunities to speak and thus can be marked separately.

Can candidates memorise some answers for the exam? While the introductory questions in Part 1 are common to all tests, candidates are advised not to prepare long answers in advance or to memorise short speeches. Examiners can easily tell when a candidate is using a pre-learned speech, and will interrupt them when they feel it is necessary to do so.

What happens if a candidate does not understand a question? If a candidate does not understand a question asked by the interlocutor, it is perfectly okay to ask for it to be repeated, even if it involves repeating, completely or partially, the instructions of one of the tasks. Candidates can always say something like *"Could you say that again, please?"* or *"I'm sorry, could you repeat the question?"*. However, should this happen frequently, it might be received as a sign that the candidate's inability to understand the interlocutor may be due to a lack of linguistic skill. If so, it might affect their score negatively, especially for *Interactive Communication*.

Are candidates allowed to touch and hold the booklet with the visual prompts in Part 2 or Part 3? In normal circumstances, it is okay for candidates to touch the materials to adjust them or bring them closer to themselves so that they can see them better. However, if a candidate decides to pick up and lift the booklet from the desk, the interlocutor will politely instruct them to put it back down so that everyone in the room can see the visuals clearly.

Cambridge C1 Advanced Speaking

Test 1

Test 1 – Part 1	Cambridge C1 Advanced: Speaking
2 minutes (3 minutes for groups of three)	

Candidates' background

Good morning/afternoon/evening. My name is .... and this is my colleague ....

And your names are?

Can I have your mark sheets, please?

Thank you.

First of all, we'd like to know something about you.

Select one or two questions and ask candidates in turn, as appropriate.

- Where are you from?
- What do you do here/there?
- How long have you been studying English?
- What do you enjoy most about learning English?

Select one or more questions from the following, as appropriate.

- How do you most enjoy spending your free time?
- How have your ambitions changed in the last few years?
- Do you still have the same friends you had when you were a child?
- Where would you like to go on your next holiday? …… (Why?)
- Do you consider yourself a risk-taker? …… (Why? / Why not?)
- Does music play an important role in your life? …… (Why? / Why not?)
- When was the last time you celebrated something important?
- Where do you see yourself in ten years' time?

Cambridge C1 Advanced: Speaking	Test 1 – Part 2
	4 minutes (6 minutes for groups of three)

1 Doing sport	2 Celebrating achievements

Interlocutor In this part of the test, I'm going to give each of you three pictures. I'd like you to talk about **two** of them on your own for about a minute, and also to answer a question about your partner's pictures.

(Candidate A), it's your turn first. Here are your pictures. They show **people doing some sport**.

Place Part 2 booklet, open at Task 1, in front of Candidate A.

I'd like you to compare **two** of the pictures and say **what role sport plays in these people's lives and how often you think they need to train.**

All right?

Candidate A

1 minute

Interlocutor Thank you.

(Candidate B), **who do you think needs to train the hardest? ...... (Why?)**

Candidate B

Approximately 30 seconds

Interlocutor Thank you. (Can I have the booklet, please?) *Retrieve Part 2 booklet.*

Now, *(Candidate B)*, here are your pictures. They show **people celebrating different achievements**.

Place Part 2 booklet, open at Task 2, in front of Candidate B.

I'd like you to compare **two** of the pictures and say **how important these people's achievements might be for their future and how they are feeling now.**

All right?

Candidate B

1 minute

Interlocutor Thank you.

(Candidate A), **who should feel the proudest of their achievement? ...... (Why?)**

Candidate A

Approximately 30 seconds

Interlocutor Thank you. (Can I have the booklet, please?) *Retrieve Part 2 booklet.*

Test 1 – Part 2
Booklet 1

Cambridge C1 Advanced: Speaking

What role does sport play in these people's lives?
How often do you think they need to train?

Cambridge C1 Advanced: Speaking

Test 1 – Part 2
Booklet 2

**How important might these people's achievements be for their future?
How are they feeling now?**

Test 1 – Part 3

4 minutes (6 minutes for groups of three)

Cambridge C1 Advanced: Speaking

Moving to a different country

Interlocutor Now, I'd like you to talk about something together for about two minutes *(3 minutes for groups of three)*.

Here are some things people think about when moving to a different country for work and a question for you to discuss. First you have some time to look at the task.

*Place **Part 3** booklet, open at **Task 3**, in front of the candidates. Allow 15 seconds.*

Now, talk to each other about **how important these things are when considering living in a different country for work.**

Candidates

....
2 minutes (3 minutes for groups of three)

Interlocutor Thank you. Now you have about a minute *(2 minutes for groups of three)* to decide **which aspect is the least important when moving to a different country for work.**

Candidates

....
1 minute (2 minutes for groups of three)

Interlocutor Thank you. (Can I have the booklet, please?) *Retrieve **Part 3** booklet.*

Part 4
4 minutes (8 minutes for groups of three)

Interlocutor *Use the following questions, in order, as appropriate:*

Do you think that a competitive salary is a good reason to move abroad? …… (Why? / Why not?)

How do you think working abroad might benefit someone's professional career?

Some people believe that having different jobs throughout their careers is important to have a fulfilling life. Do you agree? …… (Why? / Why not?)

Some people say that they would only do a job they dislike if it paid well. What's your opinion?

Do you think that a person's happiness depends on their job? …… (Why? / Why not?)

Some people find it difficult to balance their professional and personal lives. Why do you think that is?

Select any of the following prompts, as appropriate:
- **What do you think?**
- **Do you agree?**
- **And you?**

Interlocutor Thank you. That is the end of the test.

Cambridge C1 Advanced: Speaking

Test 1 – Part 3
Booklet

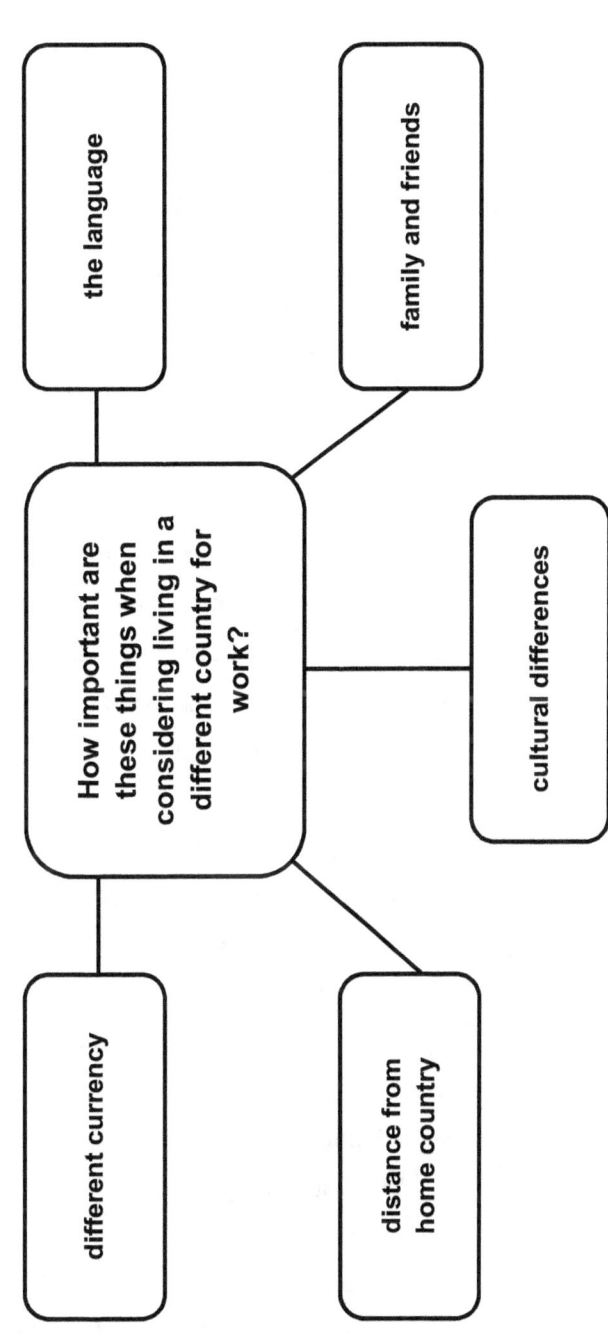

Cambridge C1 Advanced

Speaking Test Mark Sheet

Date | DD | MM | YY

Candidate _____

Marks available

Grammatical Resource	0	1	1.5	2	2.5	3	3.5	4	4.5	5
Lexical Resource	0	1	1.5	2	2.5	3	3.5	4	4.5	5
Discourse Management	0	1	1.5	2	2.5	3	3.5	4	4.5	5
Pronunciation	0	1	1.5	2	2.5	3	3.5	4	4.5	5
Interactive Communication	0	1	1.5	2	2.5	3	3.5	4	4.5	5
Global Achievement	0	1	1.5	2	2.5	3	3.5	4	4.5	5

Item descriptors

Grammatical Resource *Control* *Range*	• Degree of control of grammatical forms. • Range of grammatical forms used.
Lexical Resource *Range* *Appropriacy*	• Range of vocabulary used to give and exchange views. • Appropriacy of vocabulary used.
Discourse Management *Extent* *Relevance* *Coherence* *Cohesion*	• Stretches of language produced. • Relevance of contributions and organisation of ideas. • Use of appropriate cohesive devices and discourse markers.
Pronunciation *Intonation* *Stress* *Individual sounds*	• Intelligibility • Intonation • Word stress • Individual sounds
Interactive Communication *Initiating* *Responding* *Development*	• Initiating, responding and linking contributions to other speakers' interventions. • Maintaining and developing interaction, and negotiating towards an outcome. • Widening the scope of the interaction.

Cambridge C1 Advanced Speaking

Test 2

Test 2 – Part 1
2 minutes (3 minutes for groups of three)

Cambridge C1 Advanced: Speaking

Candidates' background

Good morning/afternoon/evening. My name is .... and this is my colleague ....

And your names are?

Can I have your mark sheets, please?

Thank you.

First of all, we'd like to know something about you.

Select one or two questions and ask candidates in turn, as appropriate.

- **Where are you from?**
- **What do you do here/there?**
- **How long have you been studying English?**
- **What do you enjoy most about learning English?**

Select one or more questions from the following, as appropriate.

- **What's the most interesting thing you have done lately?**
- **Can you tell us about something you have done that you're really proud of?**
- **What's the best thing about the area where you live? ...... (Why?)**
- **Do you prefer to go on holiday with family or with friends? ...... (Why?)**
- **Are you an avid reader? ...... (Why? / Why not?)**
- **How do you think learning a foreign language can help you?**
- **What was your favourite subject at school/college? ...... (Why?)**
- **What person has had the greatest influence on your life? ...... (Why?)**

Cambridge C1 Advanced: Speaking	Test 2 – Part 2
	4 minutes (6 minutes for groups of three)

1 Giving a speech	2 Being in a crowd

Interlocutor In this part of the test, I'm going to give each of you three pictures. I'd like you to talk about **two** of them on your own for about a minute, and also to answer a question about your partner's pictures.

(Candidate A), it's your turn first. Here are your pictures. They show **people giving a speech in public**.

Place Part 2 booklet, open at Task 1, in front of Candidate A.

I'd like you to compare **two** of the pictures, and say **how much preparation these people might have done before their speech and how they might be feeling**.

All right?

Candidate A

1 minute

Interlocutor Thank you.

(Candidate B), **who do you think is feeling most nervous? …… (Why?)**

Candidate B

Approximately 30 seconds

Interlocutor Thank you. (Can I have the booklet, please?) *Retrieve Part 2 booklet.*

Now, *(Candidate B)*, here are your pictures. They show **people who are part of a crowd**.

Place Part 2 booklet, open at Task 2, in front of Candidate B.

I'd like you to compare **two** of the pictures and say **what the people in each crowd have in common and how important it might be for them to be part of the crowd**.

All right?

Candidate B

1 minute

Interlocutor Thank you.

(Candidate A), **which crowd do you think is the safest to be in? …… (Why?)**

Candidate A

Approximately 30 seconds

Interlocutor Thank you. (Can I have the booklet, please?) *Retrieve Part 2 booklet.*

How much preparation might these people have done before speaking in public?
How might they be feeling?

Cambridge C1 Advanced: Speaking

Test 2 – Part 2
Booklet 2

What do the people in each crowd have in common?
How important might it be for them to be part of the crowd?

Test 2 – Part 3
4 minutes (6 minutes for groups of three)

Cambridge C1 Advanced: Speaking

Important changes

Interlocutor — Now, I'd like you to talk about something together for about two minutes *(3 minutes for groups of three)*.

Here are some things that can have an impact on people's lives and a question for you to discuss. First you have some time to look at the task.

*Place **Part 3** booklet, open at **Task 3**, in front of the candidates. Allow 15 seconds.*

Now, talk to each other about **how these things can change people's lives**.

Candidates

2 minutes (3 minutes for groups of three)

Interlocutor — Thank you. Now you have about a minute *(2 minutes for groups of three)* to decide **which would have the greatest impact on a person's life**.

Candidates

1 minute (2 minutes for groups of three)

Interlocutor — Thank you. (Can I have the booklet, please?) *Retrieve **Part 3** booklet.*

Part 4
4 minutes (8 minutes for groups of three)

Interlocutor — *Use the following questions, in order, as appropriate:*

Do you think that changes are generally positive or negative in a person's life? …… (Why?)

Some people feel uncomfortable when things around them change. Why do you think that is?

Is it true that the older we get, the harder we find it to accept changes? …… (Why? / Why not?)

Some people say that life is never perfect, so we always need change. What's your opinion?

Do you believe that people's lives now are more unpredictable than in the past? …… (Why? / Why not?)

Is there anything about life today that you would like to change? …… (Why? / Why not?)

Select any of the following prompts, as appropriate:
- **What do you think?**
- **Do you agree?**
- **And you?**

Interlocutor — Thank you. That is the end of the test.

Cambridge C1 Advanced: Speaking

Test 2 – Part 3
Booklet

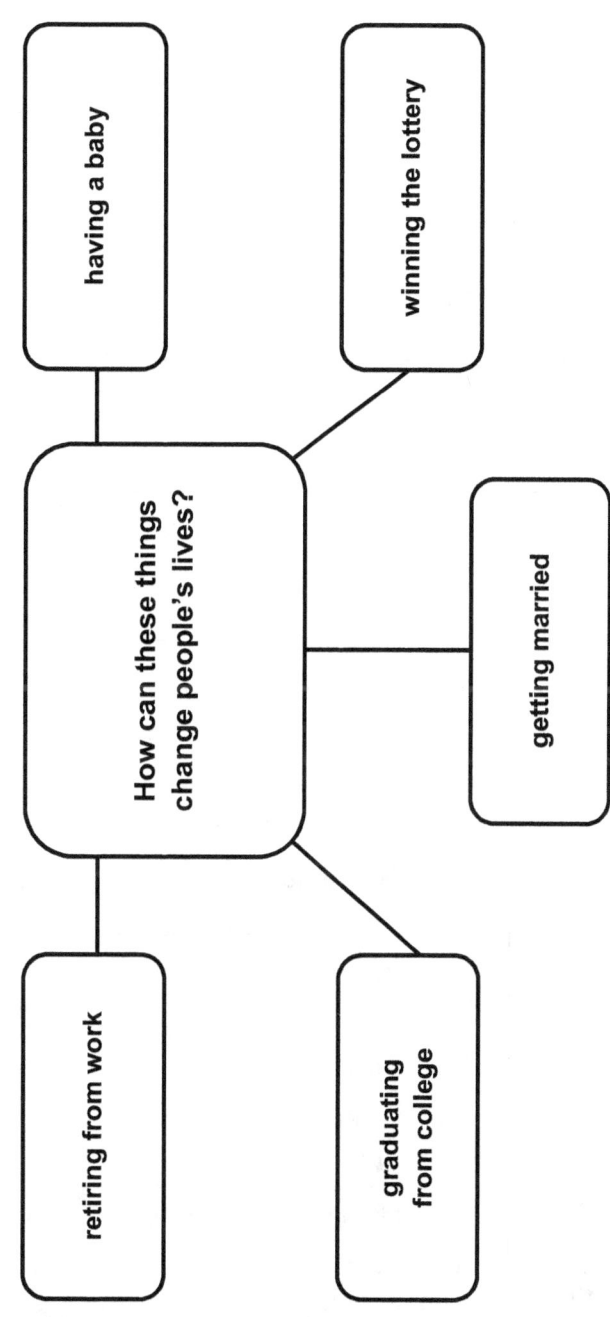

Cambridge C1 Advanced — Speaking Test Mark Sheet

Date DD / MM / YY

Candidate _____

Marks available

Grammatical Resource	0	1	1.5	2	2.5	3	3.5	4	4.5	5
Lexical Resource	0	1	1.5	2	2.5	3	3.5	4	4.5	5
Discourse Management	0	1	1.5	2	2.5	3	3.5	4	4.5	5
Pronunciation	0	1	1.5	2	2.5	3	3.5	4	4.5	5
Interactive Communication	0	1	1.5	2	2.5	3	3.5	4	4.5	5
Global Achievement	0	1	1.5	2	2.5	3	3.5	4	4.5	5

Item descriptors

Grammatical Resource *Control* *Range*	• Degree of control of grammatical forms. • Range of grammatical forms used.
Lexical Resource *Range* *Appropriacy*	• Range of vocabulary used to give and exchange views. • Appropriacy of vocabulary used.
Discourse Management *Extent* *Relevance* *Coherence* *Cohesion*	• Stretches of language produced. • Relevance of contributions and organisation of ideas. • Use of appropriate cohesive devices and discourse markers.
Pronunciation *Intonation* *Stress* *Individual sounds*	• Intelligibility • Intonation • Word stress • Individual sounds
Interactive Communication *Initiating* *Responding* *Development*	• Initiating, responding and linking contributions to other speakers' interventions. • Maintaining and developing interaction, and negotiating towards an outcome. • Widening the scope of the interaction.

Cambridge C1 Advanced Speaking

Test 3

Test 3 – Part 1
2 minutes (3 minutes for groups of three)

Cambridge C1 Advanced: Speaking

Candidates' background

Good morning/afternoon/evening. My name is .... and this is my colleague ....

And your names are?

Can I have your mark sheets, please?

Thank you.

First of all, we'd like to know something about you.

Select one or two questions and ask candidates in turn, as appropriate.

- **Where are you from?**
- **What do you do here/there?**
- **How long have you been studying English?**
- **What do you enjoy most about learning English?**

Select one or more questions from the following, as appropriate.

- **How often do you go on holiday? ...... (Why?)**
- **Would you rather be: a business owner or an employee? ...... (Why?)**
- **Are you good at using new technologies? ...... (Why? / Why not?)**
- **Can you tell us about a really good friend of yours?**
- **Have you learned anything useful recently? ...... (What?)**
- **How far into the future do you make plans? ...... (Why? / Why not?)**
- **How have your goals in life changed over time?**
- **Are birthday celebrations important to you? ...... (Why? / Why not?)**

Cambridge C1 Advanced: Speaking	Test 3 – Part 2
	4 minutes (6 minutes for groups of three)

1 People and machines	2 Stressful situations

Interlocutor In this part of the test, I'm going to give each of you three pictures. I'd like you to talk about **two** of them on your own for about a minute, and also to answer a question about your partner's pictures.

(Candidate A), it's your turn first. Here are your pictures. They show **people operating different machines**.

*Place **Part 2** booklet, open at **Task 1**, in front of Candidate A.*

I'd like you to compare **two** of the pictures, and say **how difficult these people might find it to operate these machines and how important these machines are in their lives**.

All right?

Candidate A

1 minute

Interlocutor Thank you.

(Candidate B), **who do you think needs their machine the most? ...... (Why?)**

Candidate B

Approximately 30 seconds

Interlocutor Thank you. (Can I have the booklet, please?) *Retrieve **Part 2** booklet.*

Now, *(Candidate B)*, here are your pictures. They show **different situations that can be stressful**.

*Place **Part 2** booklet, open at **Task 2**, in front of Candidate B.*

I'd like you to compare **two** of the pictures, and say **how stress can affect the people in these situations and how difficult it might be for them to remain calm**.

All right?

Candidate B

1 minute

Interlocutor Thank you.

(Candidate A), **in which situation do you think it's most important to remain calm? ...... (Why?)**

Candidate A

Approximately 30 seconds

Interlocutor Thank you. (Can I have the booklet, please?) *Retrieve **Part 2** booklet.*

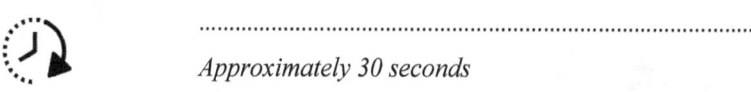

Test 3 – Part 2
Booklet 1

Cambridge C1 Advanced: Speaking

How difficult might these people find it to operate these machines?
How important are these machines in their lives?

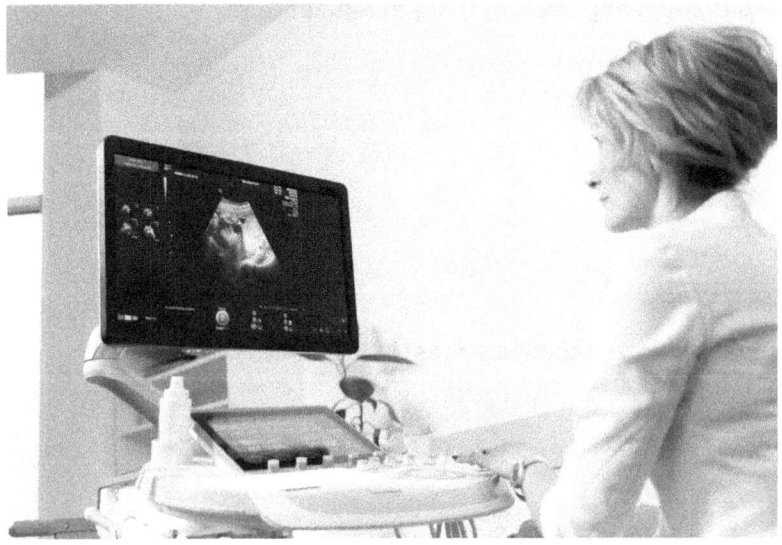

How can stress affect the people in these situations?
How difficult might it be for them to remain calm?

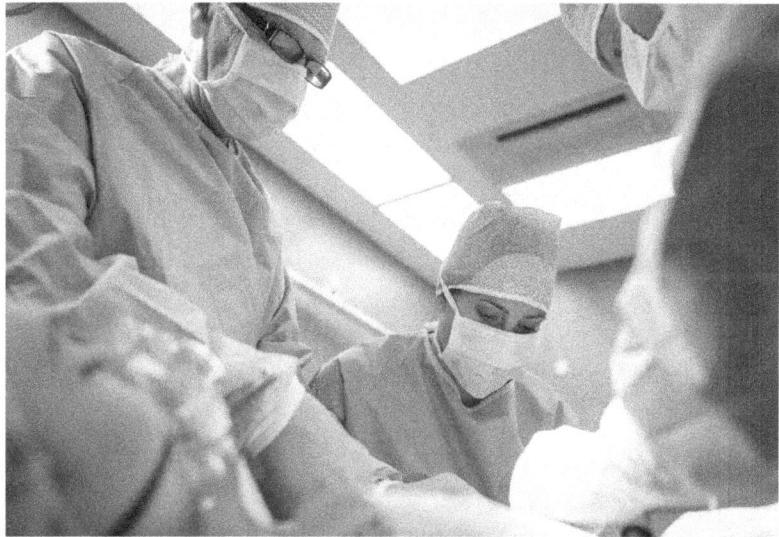

Test 3 – Part 3

4 minutes (6 minutes for groups of three)

Cambridge C1 Advanced: Speaking

Finding a new job

Interlocutor	Now, I'd like you to talk about something together for about two minutes *(3 minutes for groups of three)*.
	Here are some things people need to consider before looking for a new job and a question for you to discuss. First you have some time to look at the task.
	*Place **Part 3** booklet, open at **Task 3**, in front of the candidates. Allow 15 seconds.*
	Now, talk to each other about **how important these things are when finding a new job**.
Candidates	
	....
	2 minutes (3 minutes for groups of three)
Interlocutor	Thank you. Now you have about a minute *(2 minutes for groups of three)* to decide **which of these things people need to think about the most before accepting a job offer**.
Candidates	
	....
	1 minute (2 minutes for groups of three)
Interlocutor	Thank you. (Can I have the booklet, please?) *Retrieve **Part 3** booklet.*

Part 4

4 minutes (8 minutes for groups of three)

Interlocutor	*Use the following questions, in order, as appropriate:*	*Select any of the following prompts, as appropriate:* • **What do you think?** • **Do you agree?** • **And you?**
	Do you think that it's difficult to find a new job nowadays in your country? ...... (Why? / Why not?)	
	Some people say that, in the future, most of us will work from home. What do you think?	
	Do you think that having a four-day working week would change people's lives for the better? ...... (Why? / Why not?)	
	Some people believe that if you love your job, working will never be a problem. Do you agree? ...... (Why? / Why not?)	
	Do you believe that all jobs have a fair salary? ...... (Why? / Why not?)	
	Some people think that working hard should necessarily lead to a higher salary. What's your opinion?	
Interlocutor	Thank you. That is the end of the test.	

Cambridge C1 Advanced: Speaking

Test 3 – Part 3 Booklet

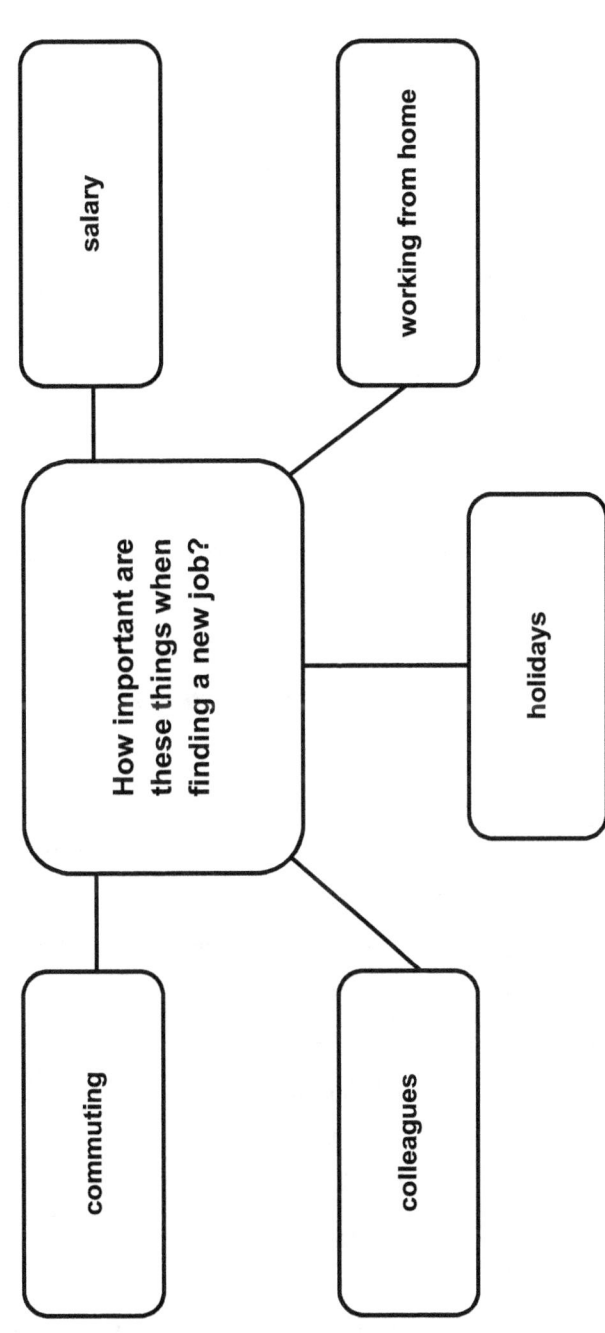

Cambridge C1 Advanced — Speaking Test Mark Sheet

Date: DD / MM / YY

Candidate: _____

Marks available

Grammatical Resource	0	1	1.5	2	2.5	3	3.5	4	4.5	5
Lexical Resource	0	1	1.5	2	2.5	3	3.5	4	4.5	5
Discourse Management	0	1	1.5	2	2.5	3	3.5	4	4.5	5
Pronunciation	0	1	1.5	2	2.5	3	3.5	4	4.5	5
Interactive Communication	0	1	1.5	2	2.5	3	3.5	4	4.5	5
Global Achievement	0	1	1.5	2	2.5	3	3.5	4	4.5	5

Item descriptors

Grammatical Resource *Control* *Range*	• Degree of control of grammatical forms. • Range of grammatical forms used.
Lexical Resource *Range* *Appropriacy*	• Range of vocabulary used to give and exchange views. • Appropriacy of vocabulary used.
Discourse Management *Extent* *Relevance* *Coherence* *Cohesion*	• Stretches of language produced. • Relevance of contributions and organisation of ideas. • Use of appropriate cohesive devices and discourse markers.
Pronunciation *Intonation* *Stress* *Individual sounds*	• Intelligibility • Intonation • Word stress • Individual sounds
Interactive Communication *Initiating* *Responding* *Development*	• Initiating, responding and linking contributions to other speakers' interventions. • Maintaining and developing interaction, and negotiating towards an outcome. • Widening the scope of the interaction.

Cambridge C1 Advanced Speaking

Test 4

Test 4 – Part 1	Cambridge C1 Advanced: Speaking
2 minutes (3 minutes for groups of three)	

Candidates' background

Good morning/afternoon/evening. My name is .... and this is my colleague ....

And your names are?

Can I have your mark sheets, please?

Thank you.

First of all, we'd like to know something about you.

Select one or two questions and ask candidates in turn, as appropriate.

- Where are you from?
- What do you do here/there?
- How long have you been studying English?
- What do you enjoy most about learning English?

Select one or more questions from the following, as appropriate.

- What do you like to do when you go out with your friends? …… (Why?)
- Can you tell us about the last time you travelled abroad?
- Do you enjoy taking pictures on your phone? …… (Why? / Why not?)
- Are you keen on TV documentaries? …… (Why? / Why not?)
- How often do you read newspapers or magazines? …… (Why? / Why not?)
- Are traditions an important part of your country's culture? …… (Why? / Why not?)
- Are you fond of social media? …… (Why? / Why not?)
- Do you like to wake up early in the morning? …… (Why? / Why not?)

Cambridge C1 Advanced: Speaking

Test 4 – Part 2
4 minutes (6 minutes for groups of three)

| 1 Taking a break | 2 Fixing things |

Interlocutor In this part of the test, I'm going to give each of you three pictures. I'd like you to talk about **two** of them on your own for about a minute, and also to answer a question about your partner's pictures.

(Candidate A), it's your turn first. Here are your pictures. They show **people taking a break in different situations**.

Place Part 2 booklet, open at Task 1, in front of Candidate A.

I'd like you to compare **two** of the pictures, and say **why these people are taking a break and how important it is that they take a break in these situations**.

All right?

Candidate A

....

1 minute

Interlocutor Thank you.

(Candidate B), **who do you think needs the break the most? …… (Why?)**

Candidate B

....

Approximately 30 seconds

Interlocutor Thank you. (Can I have the booklet, please?) *Retrieve Part 2 booklet.*

Now, *(Candidate B)*, here are your pictures. They show **people fixing different things**.

Place Part 2 booklet, open at Task 2, in front of Candidate B.

I'd like you to compare **two** of the pictures, and say **why these things are being fixed and who had to work the hardest to learn how to fix these things**.

All right?

Candidate B

....

1 minute

Interlocutor Thank you.

(Candidate A), **who do you think is finding it most enjoyable to fix things? …… (Why?)**

Candidate A

....

Approximately 30 seconds

Interlocutor Thank you. (Can I have the booklet, please?) *Retrieve Part 2 booklet.*

Why are these people taking a break?
How important is it that they take a break in these situations?

Cambridge C1 Advanced: Speaking

Test 4 – Part 2
Booklet 2

Why are these things being fixed?
Who had to work the hardest to learn how to fix these things?

Test 4 – Part 3

4 minutes (6 minutes for groups of three)

Cambridge C1 Advanced: Speaking

Difficult decisions

Interlocutor Now, I'd like you to talk about something together for about two minutes *(3 minutes for groups of three)*.

Here are some decisions that might be difficult to make and a question for you to discuss. First you have some time to look at the task.

*Place **Part 3** booklet, open at **Task 3**, in front of the candidates. Allow 15 seconds.*

Now, talk to each other about **what you need to consider before making these difficult decisions**.

Candidates

2 minutes (3 minutes for groups of three)

Interlocutor Thank you. Now you have about a minute *(2 minutes for groups of three)* to decide **which decision would have the worst consequences if made incorrectly**.

Candidates

1 minute (2 minutes for groups of three)

Interlocutor Thank you. (Can I have the booklet, please?) *Retrieve **Part 3** booklet.*

Part 4

4 minutes (8 minutes for groups of three)

Interlocutor *Use the following questions, in order, as appropriate:*

Select any of the following prompts, as appropriate:
- **What do you think?**
- **Do you agree?**
- **And you?**

Is it true that making decisions becomes more difficult as we grow older? …… (Why? / Why not?)

Do you think that young people today have difficult choices to make? …… (Why? / Why not?)

Some people believe that you should always ask for other people's advice before making an important decision. Do you agree? …… (Why? / Why not?)

Who do you think gives the best advice: friends or family? …… (Why?)

Do you think that it's always a good idea to consider the pros and cons before making a decision? …… (Why? / Why not?)

Some people say that sometimes it's the smallest decisions that can change your life forever. What do you think?

Interlocutor Thank you. That is the end of the test.

Cambridge C1 Advanced: Speaking

Test 4 – Part 3
Booklet

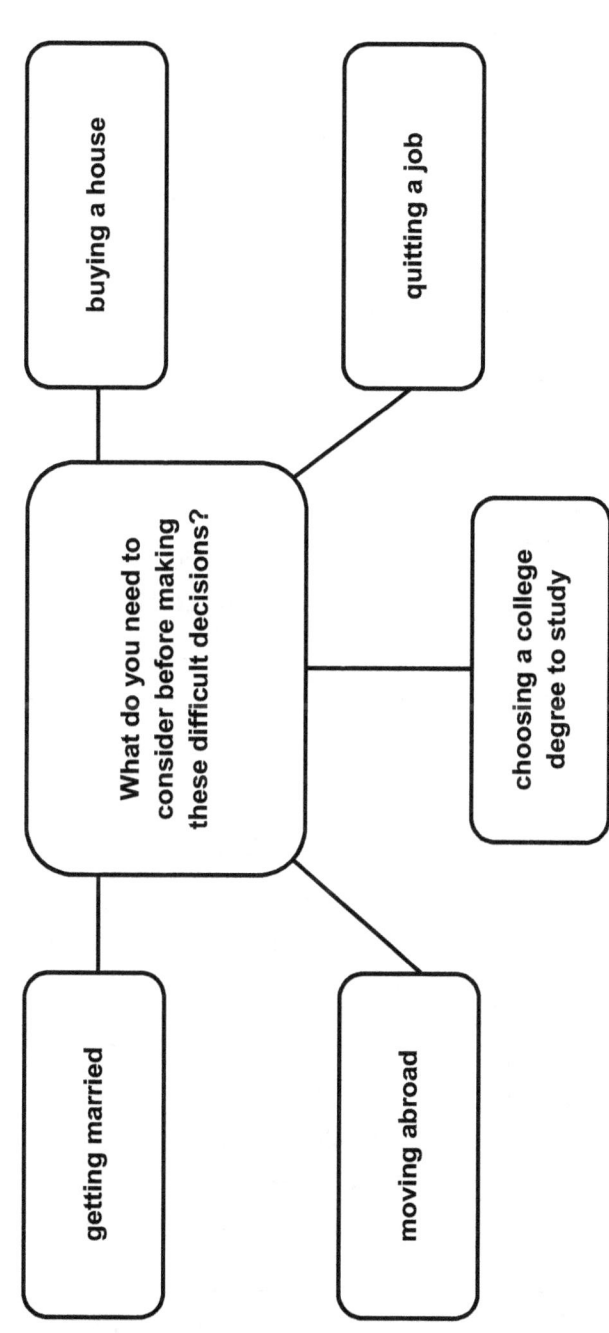

Cambridge C1 Advanced

Speaking Test Mark Sheet

Date | DD | MM | YY

Candidate _____

Marks available

Grammatical Resource	0	1	1.5	2	2.5	3	3.5	4	4.5	5
Lexical Resource	0	1	1.5	2	2.5	3	3.5	4	4.5	5
Discourse Management	0	1	1.5	2	2.5	3	3.5	4	4.5	5
Pronunciation	0	1	1.5	2	2.5	3	3.5	4	4.5	5
Interactive Communication	0	1	1.5	2	2.5	3	3.5	4	4.5	5
Global Achievement	0	1	1.5	2	2.5	3	3.5	4	4.5	5

Item descriptors

Grammatical Resource *Control* *Range*	• Degree of control of grammatical forms. • Range of grammatical forms used.
Lexical Resource *Range* *Appropriacy*	• Range of vocabulary used to give and exchange views. • Appropriacy of vocabulary used.
Discourse Management *Extent* *Relevance* *Coherence* *Cohesion*	• Stretches of language produced. • Relevance of contributions and organisation of ideas. • Use of appropriate cohesive devices and discourse markers.
Pronunciation *Intonation* *Stress* *Individual sounds*	• Intelligibility • Intonation • Word stress • Individual sounds
Interactive Communication *Initiating* *Responding* *Development*	• Initiating, responding and linking contributions to other speakers' interventions. • Maintaining and developing interaction, and negotiating towards an outcome. • Widening the scope of the interaction.

Cambridge C1 Advanced Speaking

Test 5

Test 5 – Part 1
2 minutes (3 minutes for groups of three)

Cambridge C1 Advanced: Speaking

Candidates' background

Good morning/afternoon/evening. My name is .... and this is my colleague ....

And your names are?

Can I have your mark sheets, please?

Thank you.

First of all, we'd like to know something about you.

Select one or two questions and ask candidates in turn, as appropriate.

- **Where are you from?**
- **What do you do here/there?**
- **How long have you been studying English?**
- **What do you enjoy most about learning English?**

Select one or more questions from the following, as appropriate.

- **Do you prefer to spend your free time indoors or outdoors? ...... (Why?)**
- **When was the last time you did something interesting with friends? ...... (What did you do?)**
- **Have you ever done any volunteer work? ...... (Why? / Why not?)**
- **Do you prefer to work alone or with other people? ...... (Why?)**
- **Do you enjoy cooking? ...... (Why? / Why not?)**
- **What interesting things can you do in the area where you live? ...... (Why?)**
- **How important are pets in your life? ...... (Why? / Why not?)**
- **Can you tell us about your plans for the near future? ...... (Why?)**

Cambridge C1 Advanced: Speaking	Test 5 – Part 2
	4 minutes (6 minutes for groups of three)

1 Learning a skill	2 Meetings

Interlocutor In this part of the test, I'm going to give each of you three pictures. I'd like you to talk about **two** of them on your own for about a minute, and also to answer a question about your partner's pictures.

(Candidate A), it's your turn first. Here are your pictures. They show **children learning a skill**.

Place Part 2 booklet, open at Task 1, in front of Candidate A.

I'd like you to compare **two** of the pictures, and say **how difficult it might be for the children to learn these skills and how important it is that they learn them correctly**.

All right?

Candidate A

....

1 minute

Interlocutor Thank you.

(Candidate B), **who do you think will take the longest to learn their skill? …… (Why?)**

Candidate B

....

Approximately 30 seconds

Interlocutor Thank you. (Can I have the booklet, please?) *Retrieve Part 2 booklet.*

Now, *(Candidate B)*, here are your pictures. They show **people in different types of meetings**.

Place Part 2 booklet, open at Task 2, in front of Candidate B.

I'd like you to compare **two** of the pictures, and say **why these people are in a meeting and how important the outcome of these meetings might be**.

All right?

Candidate B

....

1 minute

Interlocutor Thank you.

(Candidate A), **which meeting do you think is the most important one? …… (Why?)**

Candidate A

....

Approximately 30 seconds

Interlocutor Thank you. (Can I have the booklet, please?) *Retrieve Part 2 booklet.*

How difficult might it be for the children to learn these skills?
How important is it that they learn them correctly?

Cambridge C1 Advanced: Speaking

Test 5 – Part 2
Booklet 2

Why are these people in a meeting?
How important might the outcome of these meetings be?

Test 5 – Part 3

4 minutes (6 minutes for groups of three)

Cambridge C1 Advanced: Speaking

New technologies

Interlocutor Now, I'd like you to talk about something together for about two minutes *(3 minutes for groups of three)*.

Here are some situations in which new technologies can be useful and a question for you to discuss. First you have some time to look at the task.

*Place **Part 3** booklet, open at **Task 3**, in front of the candidates. Allow 15 seconds.*

Now, talk to each other about **how new technologies can make these things easier**.

Candidates

....

2 minutes (3 minutes for groups of three)

Interlocutor Thank you. Now you have about a minute *(2 minutes for groups of three)* to decide **in which situation new technologies might play the most important role**.

Candidates

....

1 minute (2 minutes for groups of three)

Interlocutor Thank you. (Can I have the booklet, please?) *Retrieve **Part 3** booklet.*

Part 4
4 minutes (8 minutes for groups of three)

Interlocutor *Use the following questions, in order, as appropriate:*

Select any of the following prompts, as appropriate:
• What do you think?
• Do you agree?
• And you?

Do you think that we make good use of new technologies nowadays? …… (Why? / Why not?)

How do you think new technologies will develop in the next few years? …… (Why?)

Is it true that progress in new technologies is always positive? …… (Why? / Why not?)

Some people say that technology is best when it brings people together. Do you agree?

Do you think that people were happier in the past because technology was simpler? …… (Why? / Why not?)

Some people say that it's unfair how not everyone has access to new technologies like the internet. What's your opinion?

Interlocutor Thank you. That is the end of the test.

Cambridge C1 Advanced: Speaking

Test 5 – Part 3
Booklet

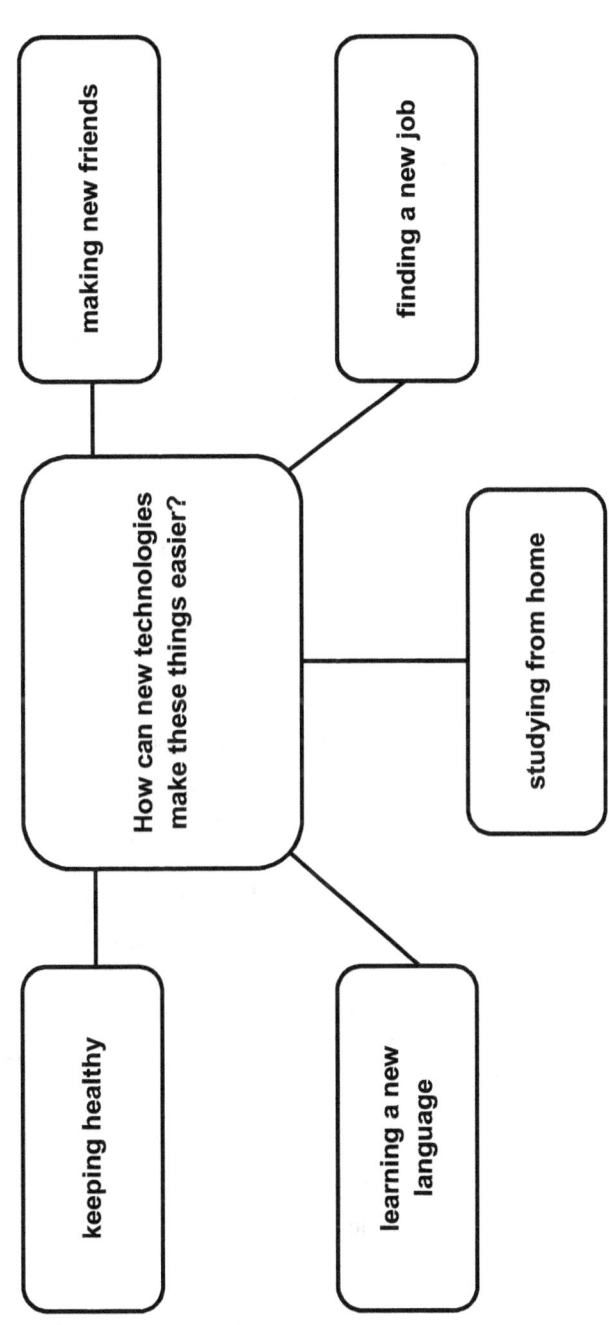

Cambridge C1 Advanced

Speaking Test Mark Sheet

Date | DD | MM | YY |

Candidate _____

Marks available

Grammatical Resource	0	1	1.5	2	2.5	3	3.5	4	4.5	5
Lexical Resource	0	1	1.5	2	2.5	3	3.5	4	4.5	5
Discourse Management	0	1	1.5	2	2.5	3	3.5	4	4.5	5
Pronunciation	0	1	1.5	2	2.5	3	3.5	4	4.5	5
Interactive Communication	0	1	1.5	2	2.5	3	3.5	4	4.5	5
Global Achievement	0	1	1.5	2	2.5	3	3.5	4	4.5	5

Item descriptors

Grammatical Resource *Control* *Range*	• Degree of control of grammatical forms. • Range of grammatical forms used.
Lexical Resource *Range* *Appropriacy*	• Range of vocabulary used to give and exchange views. • Appropriacy of vocabulary used.
Discourse Management *Extent* *Relevance* *Coherence* *Cohesion*	• Stretches of language produced. • Relevance of contributions and organisation of ideas. • Use of appropriate cohesive devices and discourse markers.
Pronunciation *Intonation* *Stress* *Individual sounds*	• Intelligibility • Intonation • Word stress • Individual sounds
Interactive Communication *Initiating* *Responding* *Development*	• Initiating, responding and linking contributions to other speakers' interventions. • Maintaining and developing interaction, and negotiating towards an outcome. • Widening the scope of the interaction.

Cambridge C1 Advanced Speaking

Test 6

Test 6 – Part 1
2 minutes (3 minutes for groups of three)

Cambridge C1 Advanced: Speaking

Candidates' background

Good morning/afternoon/evening. My name is .... and this is my colleague ....

And your names are?

Can I have your mark sheets, please?

Thank you.

First of all, we'd like to know something about you.

Select one or two questions and ask candidates in turn, as appropriate.

- **Where are you from?**

- **What do you do here/there?**

- **How long have you been studying English?**

- **What do you enjoy most about learning English?**

Select one or more questions from the following, as appropriate.

- **When was the last time you went on holiday with your family?**

- **Do you prefer watching films at the cinema or at home? ...... (Why?)**

- **Would you like to have your own business in the future? ...... (Why? / Why not?)**

- **How important are new technologies in your life? ...... (Why? / Why not?)**

- **Do you spend much time on social media nowadays? ...... (Why? / Why not?)**

- **Do you consider yourself an ambitious person? ...... (Why? / Why not?)**

- **How important is having free time in your life? ...... (Why? / Why not?)**

- **Do you like having a busy social life? ...... (Why? / Why not?)**

Cambridge C1 Advanced: Speaking

Test 6 – Part 2
4 minutes (6 minutes for groups of three)

| 1 People and dogs | 2 In need of help |

Interlocutor In this part of the test, I'm going to give each of you three pictures. I'd like you to talk about **two** of them on your own for about a minute, and also to answer a question about your partner's pictures.

(Candidate A), it's your turn first. Here are your pictures. They show **people with dogs in different situations**.

Place Part 2 booklet, open at Task 1, in front of Candidate A.

I'd like you to compare **two** of the pictures, and say **what each person's relationship with their dog might be like and how their lives would be different without them**.

All right?

Candidate A

1 minute

Interlocutor Thank you.

(Candidate B), **in which case is the dog most important for these people? …… (Why? / Why not?)**

Candidate B

Approximately 30 seconds

Interlocutor Thank you. (Can I have the booklet, please?) *Retrieve Part 2 booklet.*

Now, (Candidate B), here are your pictures. They show **people who need some help in different situations**.

Place Part 2 booklet, open at Task 2, in front of Candidate B.

I'd like you to compare **two** of the pictures, and say **what kind of help these people might need and what would happen if they didn't receive any help**.

All right?

Candidate B

1 minute

Interlocutor Thank you.

(Candidate A), **in which case is it most important to receive some help? …… (Why?)**

Candidate A

Approximately 30 seconds

Interlocutor Thank you. (Can I have the booklet, please?) *Retrieve Part 2 booklet.*

Test 6 – Part 2

Cambridge C1 Advanced: Speaking

What might each person's relationship with their dog be like?
How would their lives be different without them?

Cambridge C1 Advanced: Speaking

Test 6 – Part 2
Booklet 2

What kind of help might these people need?
What would happen if they didn't receive any help?

Test 6 – Part 3

4 minutes (6 minutes for groups of three)

Cambridge C1 Advanced: Speaking

Social media

Interlocutor	Now, I'd like you to talk about something together for about two minutes *(3 minutes for groups of three)*.
	Here are some things that people say about social networks and a question for you to discuss. First you have some time to look at the task.
	*Place **Part 3** booklet, open at **Task 3**, in front of the candidates. Allow 15 seconds.*
	Now, talk to each other about **how much you agree with these comments about social networks**.
Candidates	.... *2 minutes (3 minutes for groups of three)*
Interlocutor	Thank you. Now you have about a minute *(2 minutes for groups of three)* to decide **which comment reflects the views of most people today regarding social media**.
Candidates	.... *1 minute (2 minutes for groups of three)*
Interlocutor	Thank you. (Can I have the booklet, please?) *Retrieve **Part 3** booklet.*

Part 4

4 minutes (8 minutes for groups of three)

Interlocutor	*Use the following questions, in order, as appropriate:*	*Select any of the following prompts, as appropriate:* • **What do you think?** • **Do you agree?** • **And you?**
	Do you think that social media has more advantages than disadvantages? ...... **(Why? / Why not?)**	
	Do you think that we spend too much time on social media nowadays? ...... **(Why? / Why not?)**	
	Some people believe that minors shouldn't be allowed to use social media. Do you agree? ...... **(Why? / Why not?)**	
	In your opinion, what can people do to use social-networking sites more responsibly? ...... **(Why? / Why not?)**	
	Some people say that smartphones are almost useless without social media. What do you think?	
	Some people claim that social networks are free because they sell your data. What's your opinion?	
Interlocutor	Thank you. That is the end of the test.	

Cambridge C1 Advanced: Speaking

Test 6 – Part 3
Booklet

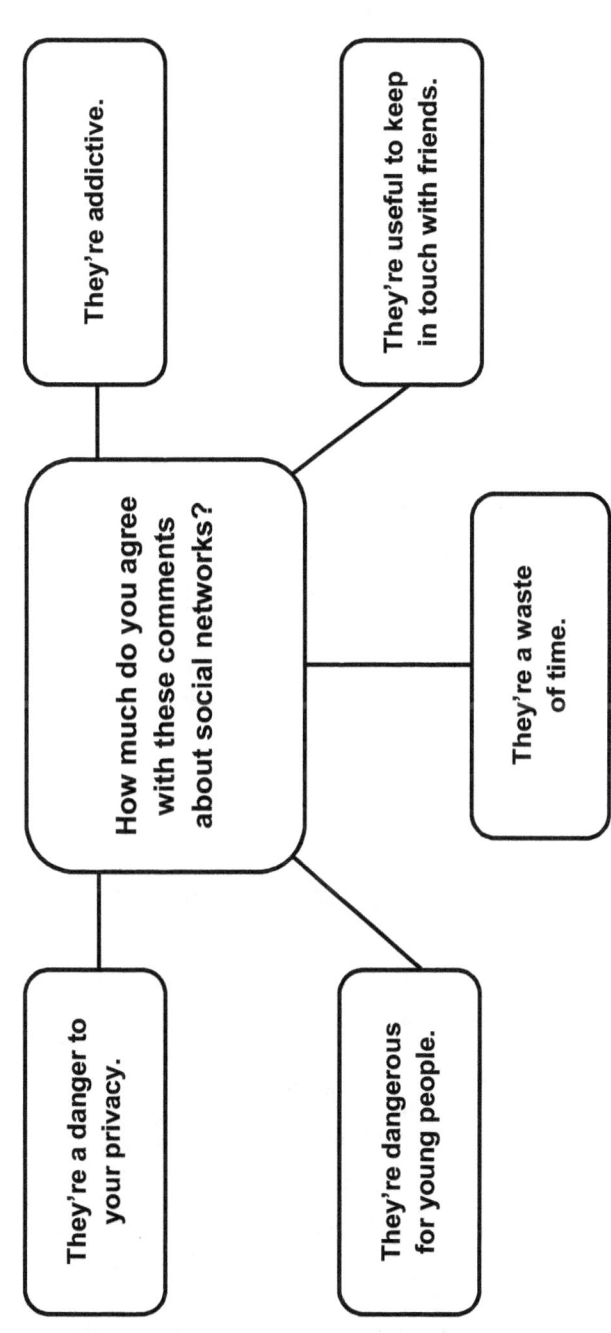

Cambridge C1 Advanced

Speaking Test Mark Sheet

Date	DD	MM	YY

Candidate _____

Marks available

Grammatical Resource	0	1	1.5	2	2.5	3	3.5	4	4.5	5
Lexical Resource	0	1	1.5	2	2.5	3	3.5	4	4.5	5
Discourse Management	0	1	1.5	2	2.5	3	3.5	4	4.5	5
Pronunciation	0	1	1.5	2	2.5	3	3.5	4	4.5	5
Interactive Communication	0	1	1.5	2	2.5	3	3.5	4	4.5	5
Global Achievement	0	1	1.5	2	2.5	3	3.5	4	4.5	5

Item descriptors

Grammatical Resource *Control* *Range*	• Degree of control of grammatical forms. • Range of grammatical forms used.
Lexical Resource *Range* *Appropriacy*	• Range of vocabulary used to give and exchange views. • Appropriacy of vocabulary used.
Discourse Management *Extent* *Relevance* *Coherence* *Cohesion*	• Stretches of language produced. • Relevance of contributions and organisation of ideas. • Use of appropriate cohesive devices and discourse markers.
Pronunciation *Intonation* *Stress* *Individual sounds*	• Intelligibility • Intonation • Word stress • Individual sounds
Interactive Communication *Initiating* *Responding* *Development*	• Initiating, responding and linking contributions to other speakers' interventions. • Maintaining and developing interaction, and negotiating towards an outcome. • Widening the scope of the interaction.

Cambridge C1 Advanced Speaking

Test 7

Test 7 – Part 1
2 minutes (3 minutes for groups of three)

Cambridge C1 Advanced: Speaking

Candidates' background

Good morning/afternoon/evening. My name is .... and this is my colleague ....

And your names are?

Can I have your mark sheets, please?

Thank you.

First of all, we'd like to know something about you.

Select one or two questions and ask candidates in turn, as appropriate.

- Where are you from?
- What do you do here/there?
- How long have you been studying English?
- What do you enjoy most about learning English?

Select one or more questions from the following, as appropriate.

- Would you rather spend your free time alone or with friends? ...... (Why?)
- Are you interested in clothes and fashion? ...... (Why? / Why not?)
- What's your favourite part of the day? ...... (Why?)
- How often do you eat out nowadays? ...... (Why? / Why not?)
- If you could visit any place in the world, where would you go? ...... (Why?)
- Do you have any skills that you're particularly proud of? ...... (What are they?)
- Do you like to plan ahead or do you prefer to improvise? ...... (Why?)
- How often do you go to live concerts? ...... (Why? / Why not?)

Cambridge C1 Advanced: Speaking

Test 7 – Part 2
4 minutes (6 minutes for groups of three)

1 In a rush	2 Passing the time

Interlocutor In this part of the test, I'm going to give each of you three pictures. I'd like you to talk about **two** of them on your own for about a minute, and also to answer a question about your partner's pictures.

(Candidate A), it's your turn first. Here are your pictures. They show **people who are in a rush to arrive somewhere**.

Place Part 2 booklet, open at Task 1, in front of Candidate A.

I'd like you to compare **two** of the pictures, and say **why these people might be in a rush and what would happen if they didn't arrive in time**.

All right?

Candidate A

1 minute

Interlocutor Thank you.

(Candidate B), **in which situation is it least important to arrive in time? ...... (Why? / Why not?)**

Candidate B

Approximately 30 seconds

Interlocutor Thank you. (Can I have the booklet, please?) *Retrieve Part 2 booklet.*

Now, *(Candidate B)*, here are your pictures. They show **people passing the time with different activities**.

Place Part 2 booklet, open at Task 2, in front of Candidate B.

I'd like you to compare **two** of the pictures, and say **why these people might have chosen these activities to pass the time and how they might be feeling**.

All right?

Candidate B

1 minute

Interlocutor Thank you.

(Candidate A), **which activity do you think is the most entertaining? ...... (Why?)**

Candidate A

Approximately 30 seconds

Interlocutor Thank you. (Can I have the booklet, please?) *Retrieve Part 2 booklet.*

Test 7 – Part 2
Booklet 1

Cambridge C1 Advanced: Speaking

Why might these people be in a rush?
What would happen if they didn't arrive in time?

**Why might these people have chosen these activities to pass the time?
How might they be feeling?**

Test 7 – Part 3
4 minutes (6 minutes for groups of three)

Cambridge C1 Advanced: Speaking

Career paths

Interlocutor Now, I'd like you to talk about something together for about two minutes *(3 minutes for groups of three)*.

Here are some career paths people want to choose nowadays and a question for you to discuss. First you have some time to look at the task.

*Place **Part 3** booklet, open at **Task 3**, in front of the candidates. Allow 15 seconds.*

Now, talk to each other about **why these career paths might be popular at present**.

Candidates

2 minutes (3 minutes for groups of three)

Interlocutor Thank you. Now you have about a minute *(2 minutes for groups of three)* to decide **which career path will become most popular among young people in the near future**.

Candidates

1 minute (2 minutes for groups of three)

Interlocutor Thank you. (Can I have the booklet, please?) *Retrieve **Part 3** booklet.*

Part 4
4 minutes (8 minutes for groups of three)

Interlocutor *Use the following questions, in order, as appropriate:*

Do you think that we always choose a career path based on our vocation? …… (Why? / Why not?)

Some people believe that it's essential to be proud of the work you do. What's your opinion?

Do you believe that having a successful career depends only on how hard you work? …… (Why? / Why not?)

Some people say that it's difficult to change career paths if you're not young. Do you agree? …… (Why? / Why not?)

How do you think our career ambitions are different from those of our grandparents? …… (Why? / Why not?)

Do you think that you will always work in the same professional field? …… (Why? / Why not?)

Select any of the following prompts, as appropriate:
- **What do you think?**
- **Do you agree?**
- **And you?**

Interlocutor Thank you. That is the end of the test.

Cambridge C1 Advanced: Speaking

Test 7 – Part 3
Booklet

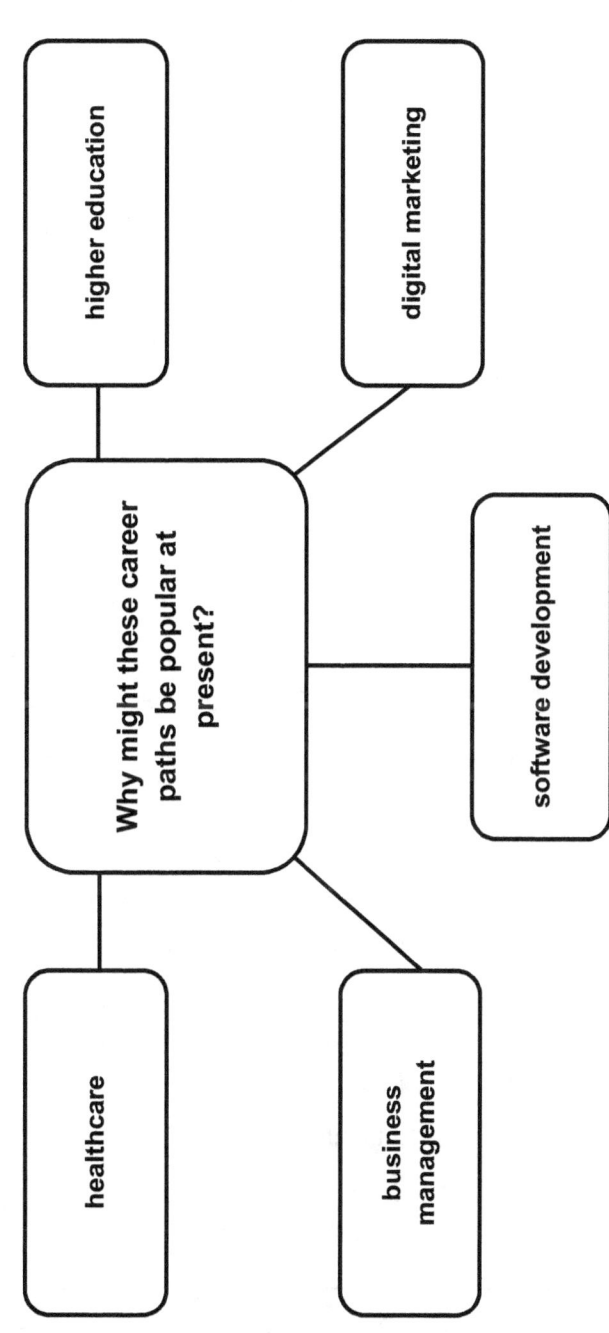

Cambridge C1 Advanced   **Speaking Test Mark Sheet**

Date | DD | MM | YY

Candidate _____

Marks available

Grammatical Resource	0	1	1.5	2	2.5	3	3.5	4	4.5	5
Lexical Resource	0	1	1.5	2	2.5	3	3.5	4	4.5	5
Discourse Management	0	1	1.5	2	2.5	3	3.5	4	4.5	5
Pronunciation	0	1	1.5	2	2.5	3	3.5	4	4.5	5
Interactive Communication	0	1	1.5	2	2.5	3	3.5	4	4.5	5
Global Achievement	0	1	1.5	2	2.5	3	3.5	4	4.5	5

Item descriptors

Grammatical Resource *Control* *Range*	• Degree of control of grammatical forms. • Range of grammatical forms used.
Lexical Resource *Range* *Appropriacy*	• Range of vocabulary used to give and exchange views. • Appropriacy of vocabulary used.
Discourse Management *Extent* *Relevance* *Coherence* *Cohesion*	• Stretches of language produced. • Relevance of contributions and organisation of ideas. • Use of appropriate cohesive devices and discourse markers.
Pronunciation *Intonation* *Stress* *Individual sounds*	• Intelligibility • Intonation • Word stress • Individual sounds
Interactive Communication *Initiating* *Responding* *Development*	• Initiating, responding and linking contributions to other speakers' interventions. • Maintaining and developing interaction, and negotiating towards an outcome. • Widening the scope of the interaction.

Cambridge C1 Advanced Speaking

Test 8

Test 8 – Part 1	Cambridge C1 Advanced: Speaking
2 minutes (3 minutes for groups of three)	

Candidates' background

Good morning/afternoon/evening. My name is .... and this is my colleague ....

And your names are?

Can I have your mark sheets, please?

Thank you.

First of all, we'd like to know something about you.

Select one or two questions and ask candidates in turn, as appropriate.

- **Where are you from?**
- **What do you do here/there?**
- **How long have you been studying English?**
- **What do you enjoy most about learning English?**

Select one or more questions from the following, as appropriate.

- **Do you prefer to read on paper or read using an electronic device? ...... (Why?)**
- **What kind of things do you enjoy doing with your family? ...... (Why?)**
- **Do you see your best friends very often? ...... (Why? / Why not?)**
- **Do you have any pets? ...... (What are they? / Why not?)**
- **Would you rather rent or buy a house to live in? ...... (Why?)**
- **If you could work or study anywhere in the world, where would it be? ...... (Why?)**
- **How often do you use your mobile phone? ...... (Why?)**
- **Do you consider yourself an adventurous person? ...... (Why? / Why not?)**

Cambridge C1 Advanced: Speaking	Test 8 – Part 2
	4 minutes (6 minutes for groups of three)

1 Ways to communicate	2 Emotions

Interlocutor In this part of the test, I'm going to give each of you three pictures. I'd like you to talk about **two** of them on your own for about a minute, and also to answer a question about your partner's pictures.

(Candidate A), it's your turn first. Here are your pictures. They show **people communicating with others in different ways**.

*Place **Part 2** booklet, open at **Task 1**, in front of Candidate A.*

I'd like you to compare **two** of the pictures, and say **why the people might have chosen to communicate in these ways and how effective communication is in each case**.

All right?

Candidate A

1 minute

Interlocutor Thank you.

(Candidate B), **which of these is the most effective way to communicate with others? ...... (Why? / Why not?)**

Candidate B

Approximately 30 seconds

Interlocutor Thank you. (Can I have the booklet, please?) *Retrieve **Part 2** booklet.*

Now, *(Candidate B)*, here are your pictures. They show **people experiencing different emotions**.

*Place **Part 2** booklet, open at **Task 2**, in front of Candidate B.*

I'd like you to compare **two** of the pictures, and say **why these people might be feeling this way and how long that emotion will last**.

All right?

Candidate B

1 minute

Interlocutor Thank you.

(Candidate A), **which emotion do you think is the most intense? ...... (Why?)**

Candidate A

Approximately 30 seconds

Interlocutor Thank you. (Can I have the booklet, please?) *Retrieve **Part 2** booklet.*

Test 8 – Part 2
Booklet 1

Cambridge C1 Advanced: Speaking

Why might the people have chosen to communicate in these ways?
How effective is communication in each case?

Cambridge C1 Advanced: Speaking

Test 8 – Part 2
Booklet 2

Why might these people be feeling this way?
How long will that emotion last?

Test 8 – Part 3

4 minutes (6 minutes for groups of three)

Cambridge C1 Advanced: Speaking

Travelling

Interlocutor Now, I'd like you to talk about something together for about two minutes *(3 minutes for groups of three)*.

Here are some things to bear in mind about travelling and a question for you to discuss. First you have some time to look at the task.

*Place **Part 3** booklet, open at **Task 3**, in front of the candidates. Allow 15 seconds.*

Now, talk to each other about **how these things might help people to choose a destination when travelling**.

Candidates

....
2 minutes (3 minutes for groups of three)

Interlocutor Thank you. Now you have about a minute *(2 minutes for groups of three)* to decide **which of these things is the most important to bear in mind when travelling**.

Candidates

....
1 minute (2 minutes for groups of three)

Interlocutor Thank you. (Can I have the booklet, please?) *Retrieve **Part 3** booklet.*

Part 4

4 minutes (8 minutes for groups of three)

Interlocutor *Use the following questions, in order, as appropriate:*

Select any of the following prompts, as appropriate:
- What do you think?
- Do you agree?
- And you?

Do you think that travelling really broadens your mind? ...... (Why? / Why not?)

Do you think that someone can be open-minded without having travelled? ...... (Why? / Why not?)

Why do you think some people choose to travel within their own country rather than going abroad?

Is sightseeing the best way to get to know a new city? ...... (Why? / Why not?)

Many people claim that some places should be protected from tourism. Why do you think that is?

Do you believe that climate change is a good reason not to travel by plane? ...... (Why? / Why not?)

Interlocutor Thank you. That is the end of the test.

Cambridge C1 Advanced: Speaking
Test 8 – Part 3 — Booklet

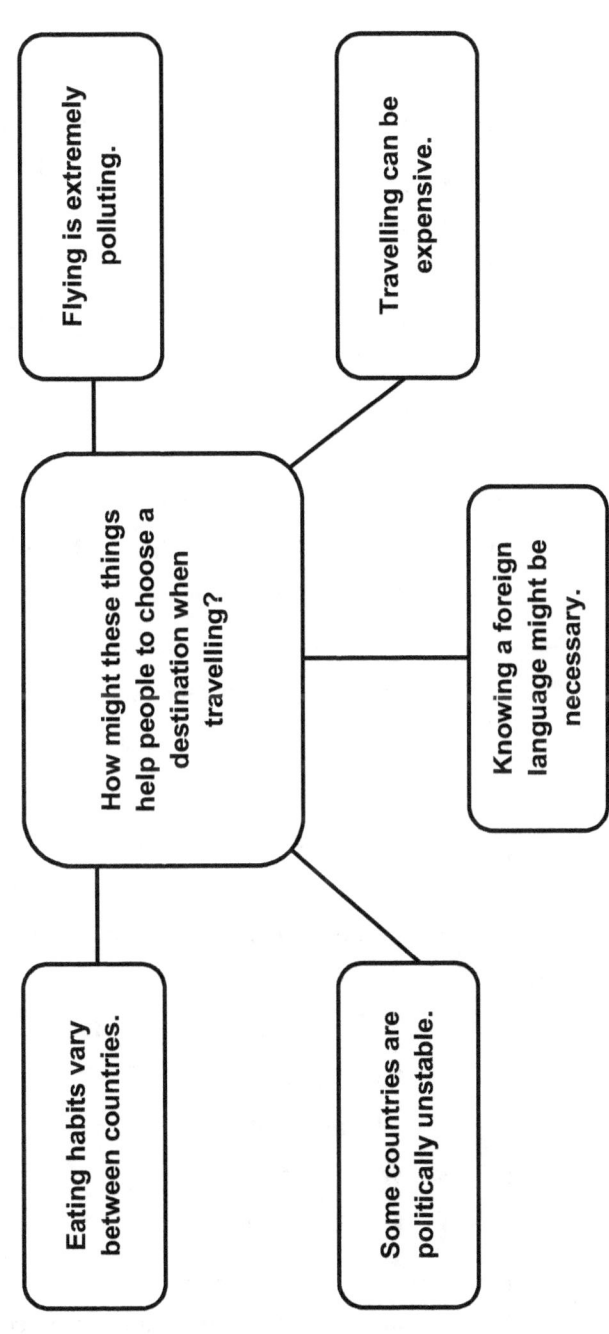

Cambridge C1 Advanced

Speaking Test Mark Sheet

Date | DD | MM | YY

Candidate _____

Marks available

Grammatical Resource	0	1	1.5	2	2.5	3	3.5	4	4.5	5
Lexical Resource	0	1	1.5	2	2.5	3	3.5	4	4.5	5
Discourse Management	0	1	1.5	2	2.5	3	3.5	4	4.5	5
Pronunciation	0	1	1.5	2	2.5	3	3.5	4	4.5	5
Interactive Communication	0	1	1.5	2	2.5	3	3.5	4	4.5	5
Global Achievement	0	1	1.5	2	2.5	3	3.5	4	4.5	5

Item descriptors

Grammatical Resource *Control* *Range*	• Degree of control of grammatical forms. • Range of grammatical forms used.
Lexical Resource *Range* *Appropriacy*	• Range of vocabulary used to give and exchange views. • Appropriacy of vocabulary used.
Discourse Management *Extent* *Relevance* *Coherence* *Cohesion*	• Stretches of language produced. • Relevance of contributions and organisation of ideas. • Use of appropriate cohesive devices and discourse markers.
Pronunciation *Intonation* *Stress* *Individual sounds*	• Intelligibility • Intonation • Word stress • Individual sounds
Interactive Communication *Initiating* *Responding* *Development*	• Initiating, responding and linking contributions to other speakers' interventions. • Maintaining and developing interaction, and negotiating towards an outcome. • Widening the scope of the interaction.

Cambridge C1 Advanced Speaking

Test 9

Test 9 – Part 1
2 minutes (3 minutes for groups of three)

Cambridge C1 Advanced: Speaking

Candidates' background

Good morning/afternoon/evening. My name is .... and this is my colleague ....

And your names are?

Can I have your mark sheets, please?

Thank you.

First of all, we'd like to know something about you.

Select one or two questions and ask candidates in turn, as appropriate.

- **Where are you from?**
- **What do you do here/there?**
- **How long have you been studying English?**
- **What do you enjoy most about learning English?**

Select one or more questions from the following, as appropriate.

- **What's a difficult decision you have had to make in your life?**
- **Do you find it easy to plan for the future? ...... (Why? / Why not?)**
- **Do you find it difficult to concentrate when you're working or studying? ...... (Why? / Why not?)**
- **Do you consider art to be an important part of your life? ...... (Why? / Why not?)**
- **Would you like to become famous some day? ...... (Why? / Why not?)**
- **When you are faced with a difficult problem, do you prefer to discuss it with friends or family? ...... (Why?)**
- **Do you consider yourself an optimist or a pessimist? ...... (Why?)**
- **What are, in your opinion, the most important qualities in a friend? ...... (Why?)**

Cambridge C1 Advanced: Speaking	Test 9 – Part 2
	4 minutes (6 minutes for groups of three)

1 Attention to detail	2 Difficult weather conditions

Interlocutor In this part of the test, I'm going to give each of you three pictures. I'd like you to talk about **two** of them on your own for about a minute, and also to answer a question about your partner's pictures.

(Candidate A), it's your turn first. Here are your pictures. They show **people doing things that require great attention to detail**.

Place Part 2 booklet, open at Task 1, in front of Candidate A.

I'd like you to compare **two** of the pictures, and say **why it is important to pay attention to details in each case, and what the consequences would be of not paying attention**.

All right?

Candidate A

1 minute

Interlocutor Thank you.

(Candidate B), **in which picture is it most important to pay attention to details? ...... (Why? / Why not?)**

Candidate B

Approximately 30 seconds

Interlocutor Thank you. (Can I have the booklet, please?) *Retrieve Part 2 booklet.*

Now, *(Candidate B)*, here are your pictures. They show **people using vehicles in difficult weather conditions**.

Place Part 2 booklet, open at Task 2, in front of Candidate B.

I'd like you to compare **two** of the pictures, and say **how the weather is affecting what the people are doing, and what could have been done to prevent these situations**.

All right?

Candidate B

1 minute

Interlocutor Thank you.

(Candidate A), **which do you think is the most difficult situation to deal with? ...... (Why?)**

Candidate A

Approximately 30 seconds

Interlocutor Thank you. (Can I have the booklet, please?) *Retrieve Part 2 booklet.*

Test 9 – Part 2
Booklet 1

Cambridge C1 Advanced: Speaking

Why is it important to pay attention to details in each case?
What would be the consequences of not paying attention?

**How is the weather affecting what the people are doing?
What could have been done to prevent these situations?**

Test 9 – Part 3
4 minutes (6 minutes for groups of three)

Cambridge C1 Advanced: Speaking

Clothing and fashion

Interlocutor Now, I'd like you to talk about something together for about two minutes *(3 minutes for groups of three)*.

Here are some situations in which the clothes we wear might be important and a question for you to discuss. First you have some time to look at the task.

*Place **Part 3** booklet, open at **Task 3**, in front of the candidates. Allow 15 seconds.*

Now, talk to each other about **how the clothes we wear might affect each situation**.

Candidates

2 minutes (3 minutes for groups of three)

Interlocutor Thank you. Now you have about a minute *(2 minutes for groups of three)* to decide **in which situation the clothes we wear are most important for a positive outcome**.

Candidates

1 minute (2 minutes for groups of three)

Interlocutor Thank you. (Can I have the booklet, please?) *Retrieve **Part 3** booklet.*

Part 4
4 minutes (8 minutes for groups of three)

Interlocutor *Use the following questions, in order, as appropriate:*

Select any of the following prompts, as appropriate:
• What do you think?
• Do you agree?
• And you?

Do you think that we worry too much nowadays about what we wear? ...... (Why? / Why not?)

Some people say that we should never judge anyone by their appearance. What do you think?

Some people believe that our clothes can show who we really are and how we feel. Do you agree? ...... (Why? / Why not?)

Do you believe that the fashion industry is responsible for our attitude towards clothes nowadays? ...... (Why? / Why not?)

Do you think that limiting clothes advertising would reduce fashion consumerism? ...... (Why? / Why not?)

Some people say that fashion is more negative than it is positive. What's your opinion?

Interlocutor Thank you. That is the end of the test.

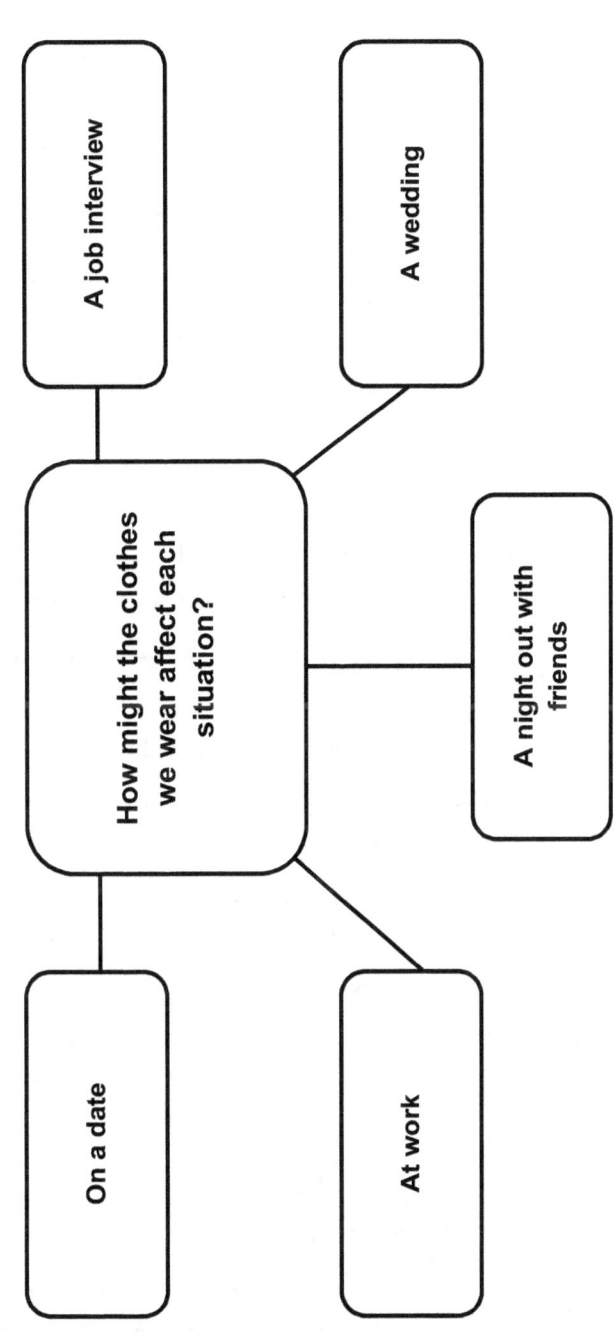

Cambridge C1 Advanced

Speaking Test Mark Sheet

Date | DD | MM | YY |

Candidate _____

Marks available

Grammatical Resource	0	1	1.5	2	2.5	3	3.5	4	4.5	5
Lexical Resource	0	1	1.5	2	2.5	3	3.5	4	4.5	5
Discourse Management	0	1	1.5	2	2.5	3	3.5	4	4.5	5
Pronunciation	0	1	1.5	2	2.5	3	3.5	4	4.5	5
Interactive Communication	0	1	1.5	2	2.5	3	3.5	4	4.5	5
Global Achievement	0	1	1.5	2	2.5	3	3.5	4	4.5	5

Item descriptors

Grammatical Resource *Control* *Range*	- Degree of control of grammatical forms. - Range of grammatical forms used.
Lexical Resource *Range* *Appropriacy*	- Range of vocabulary used to give and exchange views. - Appropriacy of vocabulary used.
Discourse Management *Extent* *Relevance* *Coherence* *Cohesion*	- Stretches of language produced. - Relevance of contributions and organisation of ideas. - Use of appropriate cohesive devices and discourse markers.
Pronunciation *Intonation* *Stress* *Individual sounds*	- Intelligibility - Intonation - Word stress - Individual sounds
Interactive Communication *Initiating* *Responding* *Development*	- Initiating, responding and linking contributions to other speakers' interventions. - Maintaining and developing interaction, and negotiating towards an outcome. - Widening the scope of the interaction.

Cambridge C1 Advanced Speaking

Test 10

Test 10 – Part 1	Cambridge C1 Advanced: Speaking
2 minutes (3 minutes for groups of three)	

Candidates' background

Good morning/afternoon/evening. My name is …………… and this is my colleague …………… .

And your names are?

Can I have your mark sheets, please?

Thank you.

First of all, we'd like to know something about you.

Select one or two questions and ask candidates in turn, as appropriate.

- Where are you from?

- What do you do here/there?

- How long have you been studying English?

- What do you enjoy most about learning English?

Select one or more questions from the following, as appropriate.

- How often do you have to write emails for work or school? …… (Why? / Why not?)

- Do you enjoy taking pictures when you travel? …… (Why? / Why not?)

- Would you say that you're an artistic person? …… (Why? / Why not?)

- How much time do you spend with your family? …… (Why?)

- Would you rather have one or several different jobs during your life? …… (Why?)

- How do you make sure that you don't forget important things? …… (Why?)

- Do you consider yourself an organised person? …… (Why? / Why not?)

- What would you do if you had more free time? …… (Why?)

Cambridge C1 Advanced: Speaking	Test 10 – Part 2
	4 minutes (6 minutes for groups of three)

1 People and nature	2 Families

Interlocutor In this part of the test, I'm going to give each of you three pictures. I'd like you to talk about **two** of them on your own for about a minute, and also to answer a question about your partner's pictures.

(Candidate A), it's your turn first. Here are your pictures. They show **people in different natural settings**.

*Place **Part 2** booklet, open at **Task 1**, in front of Candidate A.*

I'd like you to compare **two** of the pictures, and say **why the people might have chosen to be there and how they might be feeling**.

All right?

Candidate A

1 minute

Interlocutor Thank you.

(Candidate B), **which person do you think will remember their setting the longest? ...... (Why? / Why not?)**

Candidate B

Approximately 30 seconds

Interlocutor Thank you. (Can I have the booklet, please?) *Retrieve **Part 2** booklet.*

Now, *(Candidate B)*, here are your pictures. They show **family members who have gathered together for different reasons**.

*Place **Part 2** booklet, open at **Task 2**, in front of Candidate B.*

I'd like you to compare **two** of the pictures, and say **why they might have come together as a family and how important this moment might be for them**.

All right?

Candidate B

1 minute

Interlocutor Thank you.

(Candidate A), **which occasion do you think will be the most memorable? ...... (Why?)**

Candidate A

Approximately 30 seconds

Interlocutor Thank you. (Can I have the booklet, please?) *Retrieve **Part 2** booklet.*

Test 10 – Part 2
Booklet 1

Cambridge C1 Advanced: Speaking

Why might the people have chosen to be there?
How might they be feeling?

Why might these people have come together as a family?
How important might this moment be for them?

Test 10 – Part 3
4 minutes (6 minutes for groups of three)

Cambridge C1 Advanced: Speaking

| Society concerns |

Interlocutor Now, I'd like you to talk about something together for about two minutes *(3 minutes for groups of three)*.

Here are some things that concern most people these days and a question for you to discuss. First you have some time to look at the task.

Place Part 3 booklet, open at Task 3, in front of the candidates. Allow 15 seconds.

Now, talk to each other about **why these things are important for society in general**.

Candidates

2 minutes (3 minutes for groups of three)

Interlocutor Thank you. Now you have about a minute *(2 minutes for groups of three)* to decide **which of these things members of society should worry most about**.

Candidates

1 minute (2 minutes for groups of three)

Interlocutor Thank you. (Can I have the booklet, please?) *Retrieve Part 3 booklet.*

Part 4
4 minutes (8 minutes for groups of three)

Interlocutor *Use the following questions, in order, as appropriate:*

Do you think that members of society have the right priorities these days? ...... (Why? / Why not?)

Do you believe that society, as a whole, is heading in the right direction? ...... (Why? / Why not?)

In your opinion, can regular citizens really do anything to change the way society works? ...... (Why? / Why not?)

Some people say that being in good health is all that matters. What do you think?

Some people are really disappointed with politicians nowadays. Why do you think that is?

In your opinion, what are the qualities that every great politician should have? ...... (Why?)

Select any of the following prompts, as appropriate:
- **What do you think?**
- **Do you agree?**
- **And you?**

Interlocutor Thank you. That is the end of the test.

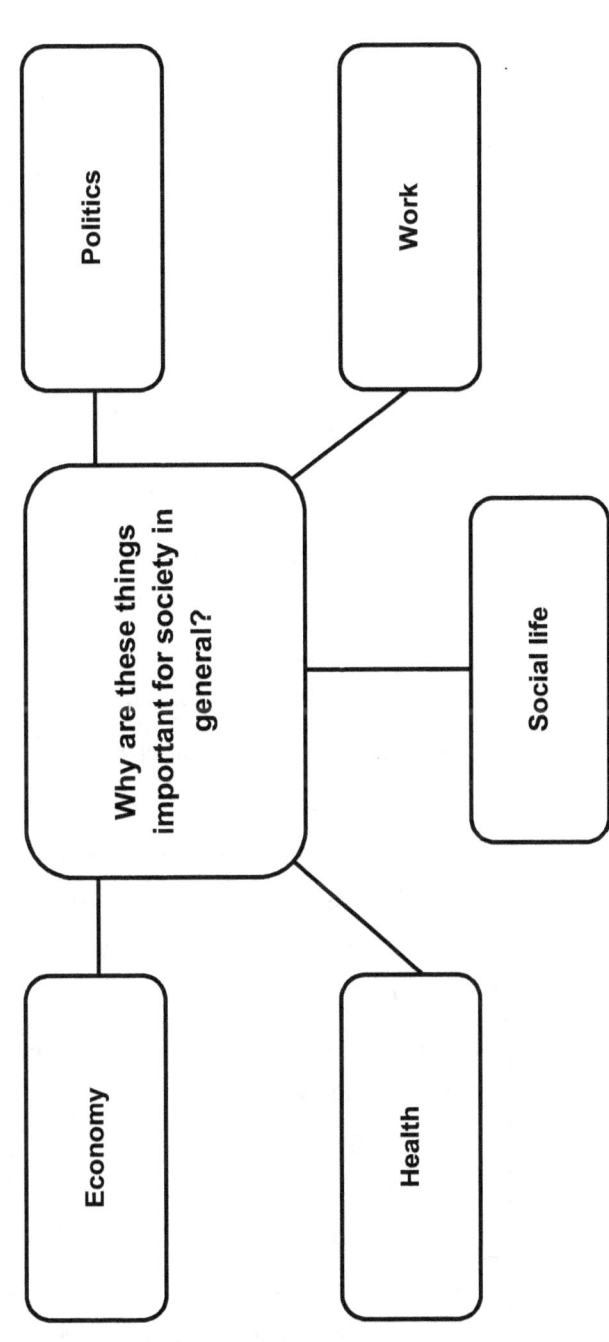

Cambridge C1 Advanced

Speaking Test Mark Sheet

Date

DD	MM	YY

Candidate _____

Marks available

Grammatical Resource	0	1	1.5	2	2.5	3	3.5	4	4.5	5
Lexical Resource	0	1	1.5	2	2.5	3	3.5	4	4.5	5
Discourse Management	0	1	1.5	2	2.5	3	3.5	4	4.5	5
Pronunciation	0	1	1.5	2	2.5	3	3.5	4	4.5	5
Interactive Communication	0	1	1.5	2	2.5	3	3.5	4	4.5	5
Global Achievement	0	1	1.5	2	2.5	3	3.5	4	4.5	5

Item descriptors

Grammatical Resource *Control* *Range*	• Degree of control of grammatical forms. • Range of grammatical forms used.
Lexical Resource *Range* *Appropriacy*	• Range of vocabulary used to give and exchange views. • Appropriacy of vocabulary used.
Discourse Management *Extent* *Relevance* *Coherence* *Cohesion*	• Stretches of language produced. • Relevance of contributions and organisation of ideas. • Use of appropriate cohesive devices and discourse markers.
Pronunciation *Intonation* *Stress* *Individual sounds*	• Intelligibility • Intonation • Word stress • Individual sounds
Interactive Communication *Initiating* *Responding* *Development*	• Initiating, responding and linking contributions to other speakers' interventions. • Maintaining and developing interaction, and negotiating towards an outcome. • Widening the scope of the interaction.

Model answers

Test 1

Model answers – Test 1

The C1 Advanced examination is usually taken by candidates who want to obtain a C1-level certificate, which corresponds to an advanced level of English. As described by the Common European Framework of Reference for Languages (CEFRL), candidates with a C1 level are considered to be *proficient users* with *effective operational proficiency*, thus being able to:

- understand a wide range of demanding, longer texts, and to recognise implicit meaning
- express themselves fluently and spontaneously without much obvious searching for expressions
- use language flexibly and effectively for social, academic and professional purposes
- produce clear, well-structured and detailed texts on complex subjects, showing controlled use of organisational patterns, connectors and cohesive devices.

The purpose of the following model answers is to provide teachers and candidates with an example of language production and test performance that would score a high mark in a real C1 Advanced Speaking test.

These answers contain grammatical and lexical features as well as a range of discourse resources suited to an advanced level of English (C1). Please note that a good degree of linguistic accuracy is expected at C1 level.

On pages 95–99, there are comments highlighting different aspects of the model answers, such as:

- the strategies candidates make use of to address some of the parts
- the ways in which candidates express their opinions
- how candidates interact with one another, etc.

The aim of these comments is to draw the reader's attention to important details that might help them to achieve a successful performance in this part of the C1 Advanced examination.

While reading the model answers and the examiner's comments, please bear in mind the following:

- The test is taken in pairs (or trios), and candidates are expected to interact with each other in parts 3 and 4.

- The approximate timing of each part of the test is as follows:

    - Part 1: 2 minutes (pair) / 3 minutes (trio)
    - Part 2: 4 minutes (pair) / 6 minutes (trio)
    - Part 3: 4 minutes (pair) / 6 minutes (trio)
    - Part 4: 5 minutes (pair) / 8 minutes (trio)

- These answers would achieve a high score in a C1 Advanced Speaking test, and so should be regarded as strong-performance answers providing examples of the types of linguistic structures candidates are expected to produce at this level rather than examples of minimum performance to pass.

Test 1 – Part 1

Cambridge C1 Advanced: Speaking

Interlocutor	Candidate A, where are you from?
Candidate A	*I'm originally from Málaga, but I've been living in Granada for the last ten years.*
Interlocutor	What do you do here?
Candidate A	*I'm an IT consultant in a marketing agency.*
Interlocutor	Candidate B, how long have you been studying English?
Candidate B	*Oh, well, most of my life, really. I think I started learning English when I was around three years old. So, yeah, quite a few years now.*
Interlocutor	What do you enjoy most about learning English?
Candidate B	*I guess that would be… being able to communicate with many people around the world. And also being able to read books and watch films in their original version. I don't like it when things get lost in translation.*
Interlocutor	Candidate A, how have your ambitions changed in the last few years?
Candidate A	*Well, if I'm being honest, I'd say they've changed quite a bit. A few years ago, I wanted to be a university professor, which is an extremely difficult position to attain, but then I landed my current job by chance and I'm quite content with it now. So, I no longer have such high ambitions.*
Interlocutor	Candidate B, where do you see yourself in ten years' time?
Candidate B	*Wow, that's a tough one. I honestly have no clue, but, if I'm being optimistic, I expect to have a better job than the one I have now, and I hope to have bought a house by then. But maybe I'm being too optimistic, so I suppose we'll just have to wait and see…*

Test 1 – Part 2

Cambridge C1 Advanced: Speaking

Task 1 – Candidate A – Doing sport

- What role does sport play in these people's lives?
- How often do you think they need to train?

Interlocutor	I'd like you to compare two of the pictures and say **what role sport plays in these people's lives and how often you think they need to train**.
Candidate A	*Each of these pictures show people for whom sport clearly plays an essential role in their lives. The second picture portrays a fit, young man running on a treadmill at the gym. He's most likely a fitness fanatic who exercises a few hours every other day. So, I'd say that sport is, on a personal level at least, extremely important to him.*
	In the third picture, however, we can see some professional cyclists who are probably racing each other. In their case, I believe sport is even more important as this is probably their bread and butter – you know, what they do for a living. Therefore, I suppose they need to train at least five or six days a week on a regular basis.
Interlocutor	Candidate B, who do you think needs to train the hardest?
Candidate B	*Well, I completely agree with Candidate A. The way I see it, the cyclists in this picture actually make a living out of sport, whereas for the other people it's more of a fun hobby or a personal choice. For this reason, I believe it's the cyclists who have to train the hardest, as they need to keep up their performance levels in order to enter and actually win professional competitions.*

| Test 1 – Part 2 (continued) | Cambridge C1 Advanced: Speaking |

Task 2 – Candidate B – Celebrating achievements

- How important might these people's achievements be for their future?
- How are they feeling now?

Interlocutor	I'd like you to compare two of the pictures and say **how important these people's achievements might be for their future and how they are feeling now**.
Candidate B	*These pictures show people who have achieved something important. The first one's of a man who has just graduated from college or university, whereas the third picture shows a young, female soccer team who seem to have just won a championship.*
	While in both pictures people are feeling ecstatic and in the mood for a well-deserved celebration, I would say that the man's achievement is probably more decisive for his future, as it will determine the kind of job he will be hoping to get soon. On the other hand, winning the football championship might be cause for celebration, but it probably won't mean as much for the girls' future, as it doesn't look like a professional-level championship, given their ages.
Interlocutor	Candidate A, who should feel the proudest of their achievement?
Candidate A	*I'd say that they should all feel proud of what they have achieved, as all can be considerable accomplishments, but I'm afraid I have to agree with Candidate B on this one. Graduating from college is a massive step forward in someone's life and, when that happens, you feel terribly proud of all the effort you put into achieving that.*

| Test 1 – Part 3 | Cambridge C1 Advanced: Speaking |

Moving to a different country

Interlocutor	Now, talk to each other about **how important these things are when considering living in a different country for work**.
Candidate A	*Would you like to begin, or shall I?*
Candidate B	*You can go first. Go ahead.*
Candidate A	*Thanks. I suppose that, when moving abroad it's important to bear in mind the distance of the new country from your own. I mean, that will determine how expensive it will be for you to come back home on holiday and, also, the time difference, which is important when calling your friends and family at home. What do you think?*
Candidate B	*That's actually a great point. I hadn't thought about that at first, but yeah, I guess you're absolutely right. And, now that you mention it, I believe you also need to take into account friends and family. I mean, it's definitely easier to move somewhere where you already know some people, whether that is friends or family. What's your opinion?*
Candidate A	*Yeah, I suppose that would make it so much easier. Also, leaving behind your loved ones can be hard. Now, moving on to the language, in my honest opinion, this is probably one of the most important things to consider before moving abroad for work. I say so because, well, it would be nuts to move abroad for work if you're not fluent in the language there, don't you think?*
Candidate B	*Oh, definitely. Yes. You really ought to know the language of the country you're moving to, especially if it's for work. And what about the currency and cultural differences? Are they important, in your view?*
Candidate A	*Well, to my mind, having a different currency isn't a big deal, as it's something you can pick up in a few days, but cultural differences... that's a different kettle of fish, wouldn't you say so?*

Test 1 – Part 3 (continued)

Candidate B	*Oh, yes, for sure. A country's culture is such a wide concept that it can take years to acquaint yourself with it. But I think it's important to make the effort to learn about a country's culture before moving there. At least, that's my point of view.*
Interlocutor	Thank you. Now you have about a minute to decide **which aspect is the least important when moving to a different country for work**.
Candidate A	*So... what do you think? Which is the least important one for you?*
Candidate B	*Well, I think we might have mentioned it already. The way I see it, the currency is something you don't need to think much about before moving there. It's something you will easily become familiar with once you start using it, and you just need to bear it in mind before you go, so you can exchange some money before heading there. What do you think? Do you agree with me?*
Candidate A	*I do, yeah. As you say, it's an aspect of living abroad that you will become accustomed to very quickly, and it's definitely not as important as other aspects like the language or, as we agreed earlier, cultural differences, right?*
Candidate B	*Yes, exactly. So, shall we agree on this one?*
Candidate A	*Yes, sure. We have an agreement.*

Test 1 – Part 4

Interlocutor	Candidate A, do you think that a competitive salary is a good reason to move abroad?
Candidate A	*Of course, why not? I mean, people move abroad every day for pleasure, studies, work, and so on, so I believe that agreeing to work in a different country in exchange for a better salary is a perfectly reasonable thing to do. I know that I would probably do it or, at the very least, consider it.*
Interlocutor	What do you think, Candidate B?
Candidate B	*I do think it's a good reason, but in my personal opinion, I'd find it very hard to do so. If you love what you do and where you live, leaving that behind can be a tough call to make. So, probably, a better salary wouldn't be a good-enough reason for me to move to a different country.*
Interlocutor	How do you think working abroad might benefit someone's professional career? *[Interlocutor prompts candidates to speak together]*
Candidate A	*What do you think, Candidate B?*
Candidate B	*I believe it all comes down to how much of a challenge working abroad is for you. In my view, if it pushes you to learn a foreign language, learn about your field and develop new professional skills, it will no doubt benefit your career in the long run, don't you think?*
Candidate A	*I couldn't agree more. To be honest, if I were an employer in a large company, for instance, I would probably want to hire a candidate who has experience of working and living abroad. Therefore, what I mean is that this kind of experience can open up some doors and opportunities that would otherwise be reserved for others.*
Interlocutor	Some people believe that having different jobs throughout their careers is important to have a fulfilling life. Do you agree? *[Interlocutor prompts candidates to speak together]*
Candidate B	*Honestly, I don't think so. We all know people who would be delighted to have only one decent job in their lives, don't we?*
Candidate A	*Yeah, certainly. It all comes down to personal preference, I believe. I mean, there will always be some people who are restless and won't stick with one job for too long, but I'm sure others are happy doing the same job throughout their entire career.*

Test 1 – Part 4 (continued)

Cambridge C1 Advanced: Speaking

Candidate B	*That's right. You couldn't have said it better.*
Interlocutor	Some people say that they would only do a job they dislike if it paid well. What's your opinion?
Candidate B	*Is it okay if I take this one first?*
Candidate A	*Sure, go ahead.*
Candidate B	*Thanks. Well, I'm certain that we have all had some jobs we didn't like that paid peanuts. So, if we're talking about a one-off gig, I wouldn't agree with that. On the other hand, if we're referring to a permanent job, something to do for an actual living, well, then yeah, it would really need to pay well if you don't enjoy doing it at all. What do you think?*
Candidate A	*I do agree with these people. I would only do something I hate if the money was good. However, I'm not sure how long I would be able to put up with it.*
Interlocutor	Candidate A, do you think that a person's happiness depends on their job?
Candidate A	*It might. I know mine doesn't, or at least not completely, but for some people, work is a huge part of their lives, so their emotional well-being might be dependent on their working situation.*
Interlocutor	What do you think, Candidate B?
Candidate B	*I completely agree with Candidate A. Some people spend too much time working and simply cannot separate their personal and professional lives. For these people, having a hard time at work might impact their personal life as well.*
Interlocutor	Some people find it difficult to balance their professional and personal lives. Why do you think that is? [Interlocutor prompts candidates to speak together]
Candidate B	*Well, I guess that, for certain jobs, it must be difficult as a worker not to think about it outside working hours or even not to put in some extra hours if you feel you need to finish some urgent tasks. What do you think, Candidate A?*
Candidate A	*Oh, for sure. In my experience, if you work with clients like I do, it's very easy to feel pressured to complete some tasks on time, for instance, which can lead to working extra hours, to more stress, etc. And, in the end, you start feeling that stress or anxiety outside work, so it's difficult to balance that with your personal life, because you feel that you should be working rather than resting or enjoying your free time, which is nonsense, really, but I know it happens.*
Interlocutor	Thank you. That is the end of the test.

Examiner's comments

Model answers – Test 1: Part 1

In Part 1, candidates are asked about themselves, their background and experiences. These questions are scripted, and the interlocutor will never improvise them. Candidates are expected to answer and justify their responses, but these should not turn into a long monologue. If the answer given to a question is particularly short, the examiner will probably ask a follow-up question like "Why?" or "Why not?". Therefore, candidates should answer more than a simple "Yes", "No" or one-word answer, but not much more. For example:

Question	Candidate B, how long have you been studying English?
Answer	*Oh, well, most of my life, really. I think I started learning English when I was around three years old. So, yeah, quite a few years now.*

In the following example, the answer might be longer than expected for Part 1, but only because the question requires a more complex response:

Interlocutor	Candidate A, how have your ambitions changed in the last few years?
Candidate A	*Well, if I'm being honest, I'd say they've changed quite a bit. A few years ago, I wanted to be a university professor, which is an extremely difficult position to attain, but then I landed my current job by chance and I'm quite content with it now. So, I no longer have such high ambitions.*

Given the nature of the conversation, these answers should sound natural and non-rehearsed. For example, notice some of the language used in Part 1 by both Candidate A and Candidate B:

> *Oh, well, most of my life, really.*
> *So, yeah, quite a few years now.*
> *Well, if I'm being honest,…*
> *Wow, that's a tough one.*

Sounding natural is part of being fluent in a language, so using some informal expressions (*Oh*), exclamations (*Wow*), contractions (*I'm; that's*) or discourse markers *(Well)* is actually encouraged, as long as they are natural and not used excessively.

As this is a C1-level speaking test, candidates' answers should show C1-level grammar and vocabulary, even in Part 1. For this reason, in the model answers provided for Part 1, there are some appropriate-level phrases like:

> *an extremely difficult position to attain*
> *I landed my current job by chance*
> *things get lost in translation*
> *I'm quite content with it now*

Part 1 is probably not the most suitable part for candidates to prove their level, but they should still try to show what they know.

Model answers – Test 1: Part 2 – Examiner's comments

In Part 2, each candidate is asked to compare two out of three pictures and answer two questions about them. Also, they have to answer a follow-up question regarding their partner's pictures. This is a chance for candidates to show how well they can speak on their own in a longer turn. As this is a C1-level test, candidates' grammar and vocabulary are expected to be excellent and there is special emphasis on their discourse management – i.e. how long they can speak for (*extent*), how relevant their contributions (*relevance*) are and how well they organise and connect their speech (*coherence* and *cohesion*).

The language candidates use

If we take a look at Candidate A's and Candidate B's comparisons, we notice that they:

- **use appropriate C1 grammar and lexis:**
  ... people for whom sport clearly plays ... The second picture portrays a ... this is probably their bread and butter ... what they do for a living ... on a regular basis ... make a living out of sport ... keep up their performance ... who seem to have just won ... feeling ecstatic ... in the mood for a well-deserved celebration ... given their ages ... considerable accomplishments ... I'm afraid I have to agree ... a massive step forward ... terribly proud ... the effort you put into ... etc.

- **use cohesive devices and discourse markers to organise their speech:**
  Each of these pictures show... for whom ... The second picture portrays ... So, I'd say that ... In the third picture, however, ... In their case ... you know ... Therefore, ... Well, ... The way I see it, ... whereas ... For this reason, ... as they need to ... in order to ... While in both ... On the other hand, ... etc.

- **describe and speculate:**
  He's most likely ... So, I'd say ... I believe ... this is probably ... I suppose ... The way I see it, ... it doesn't look like ...

How candidates organise their speech

It is also interesting to notice how both candidates organise their speech, using different strategies to approach this part of the test.

They both start by mentioning the topic that connects both pictures:

- Candidate A: *Each of these pictures show people for whom sport clearly plays an essential role in their lives.*
- Candidate B: *These pictures show people who have achieved something important.*

However, they then move on to a different strategy:

- Candidate A focuses on their two pictures separately, answering the questions and speculating about them in different paragraphs:

Picture 1	*The second picture portrays a fit, young man running on a treadmill at the gym. He's most likely a fitness fanatic who exercises a few hours every other day. So, I'd say that sport is, on a personal level at least, extremely important to him.*
Picture 2	*In the thrid picture, however, we can see some professional cyclists who are probably racing each other. In their case, I believe sport is even more important as this is probably their bread and butter – you know, what they do for a living. Therefore, I suppose they need to train at least five or six days a week on a regular basis.*

- Candidate B provides brief descriptions of each picture and then moves on to comparing both of them by focusing on the questions about the pictures:

Brief description of both pictures	*The first one's of a man who has just graduated from college or university, whereas the third picture shows a young, female soccer team who seem to have just won a championship.*

Answer to both questions while comparing	*While in both pictures people are feeling ecstatic and in the mood for a well-deserved celebration, I would say that the man's achievement is probably more decisive for his future, as it will determine the kind of job he will be hoping to get soon. On the other hand, winning the football championship might be cause for celebration, but it probably won't mean as much for the girls' future, as it doesn't look like a professional-level championship, given their ages.*

Both ways of doing this task are perfectly fine and they prove that there is not just one correct way to approach this task. However, candidates need to be aware that some comparison and speculation – rather than providing a simple description of both pictures – is essential, and that they have up to 60 seconds to provide their answers. Given how little time they have to compare and respond to the question, this should be done at the same time, as far as possible.

Follow-up question

The follow-up question is always related to the topic of the pictures. In fact, sometimes candidates will be asked to choose the most suitable one with regard to their preferences.

The answer should normally be addressed from a personal point of view, and it should expand beyond a one-phrase sentence. For example:

Interlocutor	*Candidate A, who should feel the proudest of their achievement?*
Candidate A	*I'd say that they should all feel proud of what they have achieved, as all can be considerable accomplishments, but I'm afraid I have to agree with Candidate B on this one. Graduating from college is a massive step forward in someone's life and, when that happens, you feel terribly proud of all the effort you put into achieving that.*

Candidates have up to 30 seconds to answer to the follow-up question, and it is advisable that they make the most of that time to provide a suitable answer using C1-level language.

Model answers – Test 1: Part 3 – Examiner's comments

In Part 3, candidates will hold a conversation about a topic that is presented in the form of a question and some prompts that provide ideas for this conversation. For this reason, Part 3 is the main collaborative task of the test, as it is to be carried out in pairs.

The main purpose of this part of the test is to see how well candidates can interact with each other by discussing and exchanging views and opinions, asking for opinions, justifying their answers, agreeing and disagreeing with each other, reaching agreements, making decisions, etc.

Notice the following elements in the sample answer on pages 89–94:

- **Expressing views and opinions:**
  I suppose that, … it's important to bear in mind … I hadn't thought about that … I guess … now that you mention it, … I believe … I mean, … it's definitely easier … in my honest opinion, … this is probably … I say so because, … You really ought to … Well, to my mind, … isn't a big deal, … that's a different kettle of fish … But I think … that's my point of view … the way I see it … etc.

- **Asking for opinions:**
  Would you like to begin, or shall I? … What do you think? … What's your opinion? … don't you think? … Are they important, in your view? … wouldn't you say so? … Do you agree with me? … right? … Can we agree on this one? … And what about …

- **Agreeing and disagreeing:**
  That's actually a great point … you're absolutely right … I do, yeah. … Oh, definitely. Yes … As you say, … as we agreed earlier … We have an agreement … Oh, yes, for sure … Yes, exactly … Yes, sure …

All of these expressions show that candidates are capable of initiating, responding and linking contributions to each other's turn, and that they can develop a successful interaction and negotiate towards an outcome in a very natural way.

Finally, it is extremely important that this part does not turn into two separate, individual turns at speaking rather than a seamless interaction.

Therefore, candidates should avoid lengthy answers and should try to involve their partner at the end of each turn.

Model answers – Test 1: Part 4 – Examiner's comments

In Part 4, candidates are asked questions that stem from the topic developed in Part 3. These are usually more complex questions, and they will have to answer them either individually or as a short discussion with their partner.

The main goal of this part is to produce longer stretches of language in which candidates show their ability to discuss a topic to a more complex extent. It is, therefore, a great opportunity for candidates to provide answers that are organised and insightful, and to make sure that their grammar and lexis are as good as that expected for a C1-level examination. Some examples of good answers are the following:

Interlocutor	*How do you think working abroad might benefit someone's professional career?*
Candidate A	*I believe it all comes down to how much of a challenge working abroad is for you. In my view, if it pushes you to learn a foreign language, learn about your field and develop new professional skills, it will no doubt benefit your career in the long run, don't you think?*
Candidate B	*I couldn't agree more. To be honest, if I were an employer in a large company, for instance, I would probably want to hire a candidate who has experience of working and living abroad. Therefore, what I mean is that this kind of experience can open up some doors and opportunities that would otherwise be reserved for others.*

Candidate A presents an initial 'it depends' type of premise by using an advanced phrase (*it all comes down to*). He/she then moves on to justifying it from their perspective (*In my view*) while using a first-conditional sentence (*if it…; it will…*) and C1-level grammar and lexis (*it pushes you to develop new skills; it will no doubt benefit; in the long run; etc.*). Finally, he/she ends with a question tag (*don't you think?*) which sounds very natural and shows good interaction skills by providing Candidate B the chance to chime in.

Candidate B then strongly agrees with Candidate A's view (*I couldn't agree more*) and then provides their view starting with a very natural expression (*To be honest*) and an advanced second-conditional sentence with a subjunctive (*If I were an…; I would probably…*). He/she then justifies their view with an excellent connective device (*Therefore*) and an explanatory phrase (*what I mean is that*). He/she uses a nice C1-sounding structure to end their turn (*which would otherwise be reserved for others*).

The following example also shows a great interaction in Part 4:

Interlocutor	*Some people say that they would only do a job they dislike if it paid well. What's your opinion?*
Candidate B	*Is it okay if I take this one first?*
Candidate A	*Sure, go ahead.*
Candidate B	*Thanks. Well, I'm certain that we have all had some jobs we didn't like even that paid peanuts. So, if we're talking about a one-off gig, I wouldn't agree*

	with that. On the other hand, if we're referring to a permanent job, something to do for an actual living, well, then yeah, it would really need to pay well if you don't enjoy doing it at all. What do you think?
Candidate A	*I do agree with these people. I would only work in something I hate if the money was good. However, I'm not sure how long I would be able to put up with it.*

First of all, we see how Candidate B does not just provide their answer straight away, but instead turns to Candidate A and politely asks if it's okay for him/her to answer first. Then, the answer Candidate B provides is great for several reasons:

- It uses C1-level structures: *I'm certain ... that paid peanuts ... a one-off gig ... to do for an actual living ... etc.*
- It sounds very natural.
- It is well-connected and organised: *So, ... On the other hand ... well, then ... etc.*
- It ends with a question for Candidate A: *What do you think?*

Candidate A's response is concise but correct as well. He/she shows agreement (*I do agree with*), provides their own example (*I would only*), uses a contrastive connector (*However*) and an advanced phrasal verb (*put up with*).

Finally, it is worth mentioning the presence, throughout the whole test, of collocations, idiomatic expressions and phrasal verbs typical of advanced levels of English. For example:

> *I'm originally from ... lost in translation ... I'm quite content ... no clue ... their bread and butter ... do for a living ... on a regular basis ... at the very least ... make a living out of ... keep up their performance ... in the mood for ... well-deserved ... terribly proud ... the effort you put into ... go ahead ... bear in mind ... take into account ... leaving behind ... moving on to ... it would be nuts to ... you really ought to ... something you can pick up in a few days ... a different kettle of fish ... to acquaint yourself with ... become accustomed ... perfectly reasonable ... a tough call to make ... it all comes down to ... stick with one job ... that paid peanuts ... a one-off gig ... put up with it ... emotional well-being ... dependent on ... having a hard time ... etc.*

Download the digital component

Downloadable content:

- Test picture booklets (Part 2)

Download url:

- www.prosperityeducation.net/speakingcae

Instructions:

- Go to url
- Password: TIAB
- Select the *Speaking CAE* book image
- Select content to download

www.ingramcontent.com/pod-product-compliance
Lightning Source LLC
Chambersburg PA
CBHW050718090526

44588CB00014B/2327